3

Painting with
SYNTHETIC
MEDIA

Painting with
SYNTHETIC MEDIA

Russell O. Woody, Jr.

Technical Appendix by
HENRY W. LEVISON

 REINHOLD PUBLISHING CORPORATION / NEW YORK

LIST OF ARTISTS

GARO Z. ANTREASIAN	Fig. 39.
BORIS ARTZYBASHEFF	Fig. 51. Color Plate 22.
WALLACE BASSFORD	Color Plate 6.
THOMAS HART BENTON	Figs. 36, 37, 38.
BILL BERRY	Fig. 53.
JAMES BROOKS	Figs. 4, 5.
GEORGE CHAVATEL	Figs. 34, 35, 42, 43, 44. Color Plate 19.
ELAINE DE KOONING	Fig. 6. Color Plate 3.
HELEN FRANKENTHALER	Fig. 11. Color Plate 5.
ROBERT GOODNOUGH	Figs. 25, 26. Color Plate 15.
ADOLPH GOTTLIEB	Fig. 65.
RAYMOND JONSON	Figs. 31, 32, 33. Color Plate 18.
TOBY JOYSMITH	Figs. 60, 61 (I & II). Color Plates 25, 26.
YEFFE KIMBALL	Figs. 66, 67. Color Plate 27.
NICHOLAS KRUSHENIK	Fig. 10. Color Plate 20.
ALFRED LESLIE	Fig. 69.
LEO MANSO	Fig. 56. Color Plate 21.
EUGENE MASSIN	Figs. 68, 70, 71. Color Plate 28.
ALFRED L. MELENBACKER	Figs. 57, 58, 59.
JOHN C. PELLEW	Fig. 20.
WILLIAM E. PRESTON	Figs. 18, 19. Color Plate 12.
FAIRFIELD PORTER	Figs. 22, 23.
LARRY QUACKENBUSH	Figs. 8, 9.
MILTON RESNICK	Fig. 7. Color Plate 4.
H. D. RISEBOROUGH	Fig. 41.
PAUL SAMPLE	Fig. 40.
BARKLEY SHEAKS	Fig. 17.
SYD SOLOMON	Fig. 27. Color Plate 13.
FREDERIC TAUBES	Figs. 46, 47, 48, 49, 50.
ROBERT WEAVER	Fig. 52. Color Plate 23.
RUSSELL WOODY	Figs. 3, 12, 13, 14, 16, 21, 24, 28, 29, 30, 45, 54, 55, 72. Color Plates 1, 2, 7, 8, 9, 10, 11, 15, 16, 17, 24.
MARIO YRISARRY	Figs. 62, 63, 64.

©1965 Reinhold Publishing Corporation
All rights reserved
Printed in the United States of America
Library of Congress Catalog Card No. 64-22420
Designed by Emilio Squeglio
Type set by Graphic Film Limited
Printed by New York Lithographing Corp.
Bound by Publishers Book Bindery, Inc.

CONTENTS

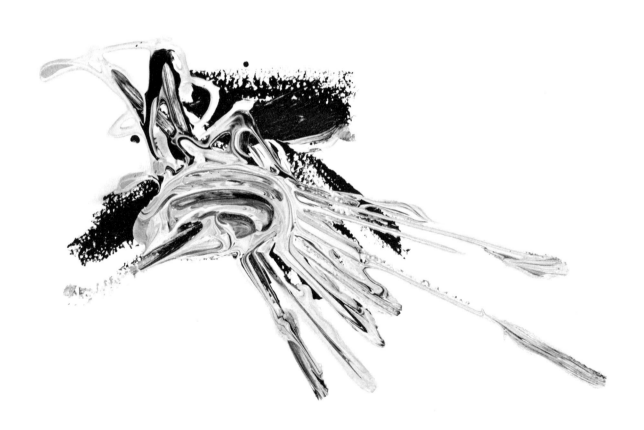

INTRODUCTION

The past decade has seen technological developments in the field of painting media that put the art world today on the threshold of a new era: the era of synthetics. This may seem a surprising, not to say shocking, statement to make in view of the fact that oil painting has dominated the art scene for the past 400 years, but in my opinion it by no means overstates the case. It is my firm belief that within twenty-five years oil paints will be all but displaced by synthetic media.

Why do I believe this? For several reasons. First, because synthetic media can be used as a *better* oil medium. That is, certain of the plastic paints can duplicate all the vaunted visual effects of oils—the rich hues, the vast range of textures and impastos and glazes, the air of "presence" and "importance" —but in a much freer and more comfortable handling technique, and with the promise of far greater durability. Synthetic paints available today are already marvelously successful in emulating oils, and still greater improvement is certain in the future. The miracle of polymerization — the chemical possibility of changing the characteristics of any substance, which is at the basis of all the synthetic paints— is sure to be developed further in the area of art media, with ever growing perfection and variety of properties.

Second, and perhaps even more important, the synthetic paints open a whole new world of esthetic expression. They have characteristics of their own that artists have only begun to exploit. The polymer emulsions particularly exhibit a luminosity and transparency of color previously unknown in any medium, and the esthetic adventures that we should see in years to come excite the imagination.

Third, the synthetics are adaptable to any art form. Not only can they be used for properties of their own or to emulate oils, they can also duplicate the sensations of watercolors, tempera, and casein. They can be used for murals, for printing techniques, for sculpture. And they comprise the first sensible material for making collages that will not collapse or disintegrate within a few years.

Finally, all tests indicate that the synthetics, when properly handled and of high quality materials, offer greater durability than any other medium, including oils, in the history of art. The pigments, protected in a medium of utter transparency, will not discolor or yellow with age. The paint film that forms over the painting is an indestructible surface that will not crack or flake or show signs of aging or weathering. Artists can truly paint for the ages.

The art world has been slow to accept the synthetics—just as artists were slow to adopt oils when they were first developed. (Almost two hundred years elapsed after the Van Eycks' innovation in oil painting techniques before oil was completely accepted as the "universal" medium.) It is a rather surprising fact that artists, supposedly so freely inventive and courageously iconoclastic, feel hidebound to the tradition of oil paints. I well understand the pleasure and satisfaction that oil paints afford an artist, but I can also offer assurance from my own experience that synthetics offer equally rich rewards—and without the headaches to which even the fondest aficionado of oils must confess.

It is not only the artists who are behind the times. The oil medium today enjoys such an entrenched position among critics, galleries, museums, and collectors that many artists who actually paint with synthetics feel compelled to label their work "oil on canvas."

And many outstanding artists *are* using the synthetics. Their influence is beginning to be felt, and the synthetics are now seen in ever widening circles of acceptance. The list of artists who are actively using synthetics includes abstract expressionists, new realists, "hard edge" painters, magic realists, and commercial artists. Among them are: Boris Artzybasheff, Wallace Bassford, C.C. Beall, Arnold Belkin, Thomas Hart Benton, Hyman Bloom, James Brooks, Gene Davis, Ernest Dieringer, Elaine de Kooning, Helen Frankenthaler, Robert Goodnough, Adolph Gottlieb, Al Held, Raymond Jonson, Toby Joysmith, William Kennedy, Yeffe Kimball, Nicholas Krushenik, Alfred Leslie, Robert Mallary, Leo Manso, Eugene Massin, Robert Motherwell, Kenneth Noland, Alfonso Ossorio, John C. Pellew, Gabor Peterdi, Fairfield Porter, Man Ray, Ad Reinhart, Milton Resnick, Umberto Romano, Syd Solomon, and Karl Zerbe.

The synthetics are especially well suited for those painters who construct their works with heavy layers of paint or with additive materials, as opposed to the simple brushing on of paint. Never before has there been so much emphasis on a painting as an object, as distinct from a representation— and never has there been so much ignorance of or disregard for the capacities of the materials that create that object. Painters pile oil paints on canvas in great globs or thick impastos up to an inch deep and then blithely paint over this wet surface—condemning the painting to early destruction by peeling or cracking when the lower layer dries some months after the upper layer. Artists glue paper or cloth to canvas, and literally throw mixtures of paint and sand or other additives onto a work. Glazes or washes of paint are often brushed on over the built-up texture, and they are totally inadequate to do the job of sealing the additives for any length of time. The synthetics, with their fast drying time and excellent adhesive qualities, could permit such dramatic manners of expression without the danger of early disintegration.

To a certain extent, the behavior of the synthetic paints requires new methods of working by the artist. In general, these techniques are easier than with traditional media, and they minimize the artist's concern about technical or mechanical matters. But this does not mean that there are *no* rules for painting with synthetics. There are, and the artist must know them well if he is going to make his tools work for him and not against him.

The purpose of this book is to explain the nature and the behavior of the synthetic paints, to survey the varieties available to the artist, to discuss how these paints may be used in actual operation, and to illustrate their diverse manipulations. I have studied and researched all the paint brands mentioned in this book—and have personally painted with most of them. By way of illustration, my own paintings and the works of many prominent artists are reproduced, and the specific technical methods of media application are described in some detail. This information was gathered from the artists themselves, either in discussion or in written descriptions. I would like to thank these artists for their help, their time, and their enthusiasm in this project.

The techniques described need not be the only ones the artist may employ, however. The potentials of the synthetics have only begun to be exploited, and I would encourage the reader— once he has a basic understanding of the composition, behavior, and physical characteristics of the synthetics—to explore and experiment for himself.

PART I
THE RISE OF SYNTHETIC MEDIA

Chapter 1 / A Brief History of Painting Media

In the history of art, there is a marked—though hardly surprising—correlation between the discovery of a new physical medium and the rise of a new form of expression. Every medium has its own characteristics—its own methods of handling, its own degree of transparency or opacity, its own range of possible effects, its own unique surface appearance. These qualities of media have had perhaps as much to do with the changing expressions and schools and styles of art through the ages as did the changing intellectual climate or changing esthetic tastes. This was certainly true at least until oil painting became firmly lodged as *the* important medium by the seventeenth century; oil is so flexible a vehicle that it permitted a vast range and panorama of styles within one medium.

The new synthetic paints afford an opportunity for a further extension of artistic expression. Just as in the past, new art forms grew out of new material means of expression, new synthetics may well herald new forms in art as dramatic as those brought about by the development of oil paints.

Cave Painting to the Christian Era

Cave Paintings. The earliest paintings extant date from the Ice Age and are found in the cave dwellings of Spain and southern France. They were probably painted with a mixture of natural pigment and human or animal gum—such as spittle mixed with colored clays and charred wood. These cave paintings, which are amazingly realistic depictions of wild game and small animals, were supposedly done for religious or magic purposes to assure successful hunting. They were not done for the purpose of decorating walls, or indeed for any long-range purpose. This belief is attested to by the fact that they were usually found deep within dark caves and were many times superimposed, one painting on top of another, without any apparent attempt at comprehensive design. The survival of the cave paintings thus cannot be ascribed to the artist's intention to preserve his works for posterity, but to nature's fortunate intervention. These paintings have been preserved by a coating of silicates deposited over them by the slow seepage of water and minerals (in much the same manner as Pre-Columbian frescoes in Mexico were preserved). (It is interesting to note that some of the earliest attempts to paint with synthetics began with the use of paint chemically produced from silicates—the same basic materials that protected primitive paintings for so many eons. These experiments began in 1825, and by 1923 the silicon esters were being used as stone preservatives and by the late 1920s as mural painting media.)

Egypt. The famous Egyptian tomb paintings used a simple watercolor technique applied to mud plaster walls. The paintings, essentially religious in purpose, were intended to help carry the dead person's worldly comforts and happiness into the after-life. The watercolor media, handled in a linear style and in flat color tones, and sometimes augmented with engraved designs, enabled the artist to depict persons and objects in their most characteristic positions, although they were drawn in stylized forms and reduced to the simplest visual aspects, generally in profile.

The Egyptian paintings have been preserved because of the dry desert climate and because they were sealed in tombs which were protected from humidity and any type of atmospheric deterioration. The touch of a damp sponge would destroy many of these delicate paintings.

Greece. The encaustic medium used by the Greeks to decorate architecture probably achieved a high degree of technical development, though none of the paintings are known to exist and no records have been found of the artists' exact methods. In encaustic painting, pigment was mixed with a wax medium, then heated and applied to the intended surface—usually a wall. On completion, the picture was heated by passing a warm metal plate over the surface to bring the wax to the top; this served the same protective purpose as varnish does today.

This technique declined with the Roman conquest and was ultimately lost, because no efforts were made to preserve paintings. It was a Greek theory that the highest purpose of any art is utility, and painting was considered a minor art somewhere below the level of basket weaving. Painting was used as a decorative adjunct to architecture, to expand the limits of a wall and to fool the eye.

The Medieval Era

Tempera. From its beginnings in Early Christian and Byzantine art, tempera painting was the chief method employed by artists until the development of oil painting by Jan and Hubert Van Eyck in the early fifteenth century. In tempera painting, colors are mixed with a type of glue medium, either animal (egg) or vegetable (gums such as gum arabic), which is diluted with water.

As used in Medieval times, the tempera process was a brilliant and relatively permanent medium, but it was very difficult to handle. It had to be painted in flat patterns, with little or no blending of colors, because of the rapid evaporation of water and the absorbent surface of the gesso ground. Modeling could be achieved only by cross-hatching of lines drawn in ink beneath the tempera. Thus the Medieval artists were mainly concerned with abstract, almost geometric, patterns.

The Medieval artists felt little need to develop a more flexible medium because the Church fixed certain canons for painting and decoration of almost every type, from which the artist was not allowed to deviate.

Fresco. Fresco, which was also used in the Medieval period, is the technique of painting on wet lime plaster with colors ground in limewater. The lime both acts as a binder medium and protects the pigments by forming a crystalline film of lime on the surface. Like tempera, fresco is a tedious process in that color is applied to small portions of wet plaster which can only be painted within a day's time. Each day fresh plaster must be applied. Corrections cannot be made unless the plaster is taken off and reapplied.

Like tempera, fresco suited the esthetics of the time because it lent itself well to flat decorative patterns. However, Michelangelo's dramatically flowing frescos in the Sistine Chapel were done with a very different esthetic intent, and show the medium's versatility in the hands of a genius.

The Development of an Oil Medium

In Medieval Times. The twelfth century historian, Theophilus, Monk of Paderborn, mentions oil painting that was not very different from the oil paints we use today: pigment ground in oil (some historians, indeed, believe that a form of oil painting was done even before that time). But it was apparently not used very much. The oils at that time were crude and thick, and thinners were almost unknown. Also, the painters, accustomed to the fast-drying tempera medium, apparently did not like to wait so long for oil to dry before overpainting.

Van Eyck. Around 1410, Hubert Van Eyck, looking for a varnish to cover his tempera paintings which would not crack when exposed to the sun, began to experiment with what can be called the first successful oil medium; or so the legend goes. The varnish commonly used at the time—a type of boiled linseed oil or walnut oil with resin added—was so thick it had to be spread on by hand, and it was very dark in color. In order to thin the varnish, Van Eyck added an essential oil (such as turpentine) to the cooked oil, and he is believed by some historians to have mixed in other ingredients too, the nature of which is no longer known.

Van Eyck possibly used his medium in a tempera oil emulsion. Mixing the combined tempera and oil emulsion with pigment, he could have painted into a coating of his boiled oil and his thinner while the oil was wet. He still painted in the tempera technique, however, first drawing in the composition with inks, indicating the shadows by cross-hatching. This type of underdrawing in monochrome (or in complementary or local colors) allows for quick completion of a painting as opposed to oil underpainting which, even done thinly, takes an inappropriate amount of time to dry for overpainting. The underpainting in tempera into the oil coating also increases the luminosity of oil glazes used to finish the painting.

Van Eyck most probably began to use oil glazes over a white ground without the tempera. For example: glazes of yellow and blue, one over the other, produce a brilliant third color of green—an idea which came from his experience in stained glass windows.

This method of oil painting led to the approximation of visual reality as the artist became fascinated by the exact modeling, the blending, the almost photographic effects to which the medium lent itself. Thus the abstract design which tempera painting fostered was forgotten.

The Italians, Fifteenth and Sixteenth Centuries. The Renaissance had already begun when Antonello da Messina and Justus van Gent introduced the oil technique to Italy in the mid-fifteenth century. The civilized world was taking a new look at itself, the Church had relaxed its grip on ideas and behavior, and experimentation and reexamination were the order of the day. The atmosphere was ideal for the development of a new art medium, especially one whose touchstone was freedom of expression, and artists embraced the oil medium with great excitement and growing mastery till it reached its zenith with the High Renaissance.

The exact contents of the oil paints used in the fifteenth century are not known, but materials such as leaded oils and soft and hard resins and varnishes have been suggested by historians as additives. Whatever the exact media, they worked well. Pigments were ground each day in oil, making a fresh supply of paints each day, and the artist painted directly on a prepared ground. The speed with which oil paint could be applied made the act of painting a very different experience from the laborious tempera and fresco techniques. The artist could experiment directly on the canvas rather than have to plan a picture in its totality before beginning its creation. The fluidity of the medium permitted a variety of effects within a single picture. Areas could be handled in broad, flowing treatment, or the precise details of Van Eyck could be produced. Glazes and heavy impastos were facilitated with equal ease. The medium evidently dried relatively quickly, permitting easy reworking.

Not all of the many experiments attempted in these early years of oils were successful, of course. Some of Leonardo da Vinci's efforts, for example, in which he is believed to have introduced wax to the media, have proved disastrous. But the Italian Renaissance remains the fountainhead for the rich wealth of form and beauty that the oil media has given the world.

Peter Paul Rubens. The Italian oil medium and techniques were further developed in Flanders by Peter Paul Rubens and by other Dutch painters of the early seventeenth century into one of the most versatile oil vehicles artists have ever had at their command. It was also one of the most durable. In Rubens' work, every brush stroke still stands up today. The paintings are luminous in quality and have yellowed only slightly. Even the impastos and the dark shadows retain their original colors to a degree that is rare for such a relatively thick medium as Rubens used.

Rubens probably made his medium by grinding pigments thickly with heated or sun-thickened linseed oil or nut oil, to which resin (hard or soft) was added. (A raw linseed oil would never have produced Rubens' delicate glazes and heavy opaque brush work and still retained the clear colors and crisp, heavy whites evident in his paintings today.) Venice turpentine, as well as gum turpentine, was probably used to give the medium fluidity. (Several historical sources record that he was opposed to using oil of spike, then in common use for

thinning purposes.) Rubens constructed his paintings with infinite care, handling each color and each degree of desired thickness in the manner dictated by the physical facts of paints. His turpentine-thinned medium could be used to give the vehicle a dragging quality. Thick glazes could be rubbed on with the thumb or the ball of the hand. Rubens painted the darker areas transparently with thin washes of color. The light areas, in contrast, were of heavy body and afterwards softened with glazes.

Rubens' turpentine-thinned paints improved the oil medium in many ways: they achieved greater facility in handling, and a greater degree of color blending on the canvas; drying time was relatively fast, and durability and lasting freshness of color were greatly increased. Rubens' paintings were so rich in oil content that they did not require varnishing for many years.

Rubens' medium was used in slightly different forms, and to varying effects, until the end of the seventeenth century. Such artists as Titian and Velasquez (the latter studied with Rubens for a short time) freely imitated Rubens' manner and technique of working in the medium. The "Dutch Little Masters" applied the thinned oil resin for a delicate effect, while Rembrandt used the medium with much impasto.

The Decline of Oil Media

Rubens represented the high point of oil painting in terms of sheer craftsmanship. From his death on, the technique of oil painting is a history of slow decline. In the time of the Old Masters, painting methods and techniques were learned in the workshops and artists' guilds. Each master made additions and changed formulas of oil methods to suit his particular needs and to perfect the medium. He passed his knowledge on to an apprentice, who was usually many years in learning his trade. This process of apprenticeship gave the artist a sound working knowledge of the craft that goes into making a painting; the craft became "second nature." The apprentice knew exactly what materials went into a paint, because he made it. He learned the behavior—the "laws"—of the various oils, the

various pigments, the various resins and thinners. It was such intimate knowledge as to how to construct a painting, and not a lost "secret" formula, that explains the longevity of the masterpieces of the fifteenth, sixteenth and seventeenth centuries.

The great developments in science and industry in the eighteenth and nineteenth centuries released the artist from the labor of making his own materials—and with that release came the loss of "second nature" knowledge of technique. When ready-made tube colors were introduced in the first half of the nineteenth century, the artist's divorce from his materials became all but complete.

In the industrially made paints, pigments were ground in pure raw oil, and they are still today. The artist adds only turpentine. But pure raw oil in itself is not adequate to preserve a painting. The Old Masters tried to protect and hold pigments by employing such binders as stand oils or sun-thickened oils, perhaps with resins. These had great affinity for pigment particles and were good wetting agents. Raw oil is relatively poor in these respects, and it does not dry to the strong, glossy films characteristic of stand oil, sun-thickened oil, or oil-resin varnishes. And so, while paintings by Rubens and Titian and Velasquez are still in good condition, and some Rembrandts are only just beginning to show fine spider-web cracking, we watch the gradual disintegration of more recent paintings by Chardin, Delacroix, Renoir and Manet.

And today the craft seems to be at its lowest ebb as we observe the peeling, blistering collapse of many modern paintings some ten years after they were painted. Such early demises are not the fault of the commercial paints, but are rather due to ignorance of basic painting craftsmanship. Artists of the past did not separate the idea of craft from their artistic aims; the two went hand in hand, the artist using his materials in ways he knew they could be used—not just for an immediate effect but for a lasting achievement. While the Old Masters considered their materials aides and allies to their esthetic intent, many artists today seem to feel that to become too immersed in the physical aspects of painting will hinder the free flow of their artistic expression.

Surely the fact is the opposite; the more an artist knows about technique the less he is hampered by it. The more cognizant an artist is of his materials, the more he is able to transcend them. If oil painting is the only method satisfying to an artist, he must study the limitations and advantages of oil and adapt it to his purposes, as the Old Masters did. There are many excellent books on this subject. The best are Max Doerner's *The Materials of the Artist and Their Use in Painting, with Notes on the Techniques of the Old Masters;* Frederic Taubes' *The Technique of Oil Painting* (seventeenth edition); Martin J. Fischer's *The Permanent Palette;* and Ralph Mayer's *The Artist's Handbook of Materials and Techniques.*

Oil all but replaced tempera and fresco painting because it gave the artist a medium that he could employ to realize an infinitely greater range of esthetic effects with much less labor. The new synthetics promise the artist a still more versatile and trouble-free medium. We are now at about the stage with synthetics that Hubert Van Eyck was when he developed oil as a medium: he continued using it in a more or less tempera method, and had no inkling of the breathtaking panorama of forms and effects which were to come. Most artists today employ synthetics as an easier way to achieve the effects of oils—and the synthetics accomplish this objective very well indeed. Many artists are already finding new possibilities in esthetic form and expression with the synthetics. Who knows what the future holds when these possibilities are fully exploited?

Chapter 2 / Advantages of the Synthetic Media

The Structure of Paint. All artists' paints, from tempera to oil to watercolor to synthetics, are composed of two essential ingredients; *pigment*, which is a dry, powdery substance that provides the color in a painting; and *medium*, which is a liquid vehicle by which pigment is applied and adhered to a surface. (Other materials are often added to paints for a variety of reasons, to give body and fluidity, to achieve matte or gloss effects, etc., but pigments and media are the essentials.)

Traditional paints, such as oils and watercolors, use natural materials for media. Linseed oil, the basis for most oil media, is an oil pressed from the seeds of the flax plant and purified for use. The synthetic paints, however, use artificially created chemical products for media.

Basic Requirements of a Medium. Pigments may be considered the substance or the objective of a painting, and medium, as its name implies, is a means to an end. All media must meet a certain basic list of requirements in order to serve the pigment well, to perform satisfactorily in application, and to preserve the life of a painting. These requirements are:

1. The medium must be sufficiently transparent in itself so as not to change the colors of the pigments. The medium should not discolor with age.

2. When pigment is ground and mixed with the medium, the pigment must be completely and evenly dispersed—"suspended"—in the medium. The medium must maintain this suspension as the paint dries, and not permit the pigment to run together or separate from the medium.

3. The medium should protect the pigment by forming a film over the pigments as the paint dries.

4. This film should allow for expansion and contraction of the paint caused by temperature and humidity changes, so the paint will not crack.

5. The paint must afford good "handling" qualities. It should be versatile in application, and respond readily to the artist's wishes.

6. The medium should be a strong binder, adhering well to the canvas or other support used for a painting, and it should maintain this adhesion for unlimited time.

The history of art media, as outlined in the previous chapter, is basically a search for improved media that would afford superior qualities in one or more of the above requirements. Oil paints, until a few years ago, represented the highest point in that search. But oils still fell short of an "ideal" medium: that is, one that offers the most acute response to the artist's esthetic intentions and guarantees unlimited life as well.

Drawbacks of the Oil Medium. The oil medium darkens and yellows with age, and cracks often develop in the film. From the handling standpoint, the greatest technical problem for the artist in using oil paints is presented by its slow drying time. In one sense, the slow drying process is advantageous in that it permits blending of colors on the canvas. If artists today were accustomed to handling oil paints in the slow and gradual manner of the Old Masters, the slow drying time would be no handicap. But ours is an impatient age, and one of the basic esthetic tenets of many painters today is that the *act* of painting is crucial to a work's impact or "meaning." "Accidental" effects such as unplanned runs or masses of paint that occur in the process of applying the paint often become an integral part of the work of art. And the artist is supposed to work fast in order to achieve the highest and purest expression. This is a very interesting and valuable approach to art, but oil paint is not the medium to accomplish it; at least if the artist wishes his painting to last, to be more than an immediate expression of his immediate esthetic impulses.

The drying of oil is a slow, continuing chemical reaction of oxidation and polymerization. By the absorption of oxygen from the air, a series of chemical reactions are initiated that convert the

13

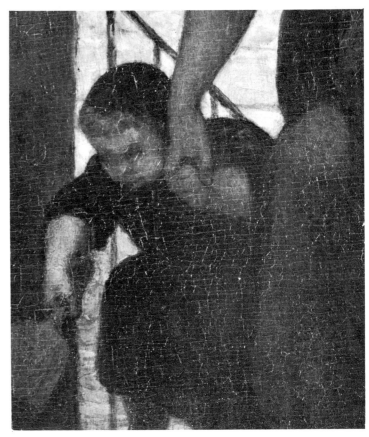

oil to a solid "linoxyn," which forms the paint film and protects the pigments. Although some artists occasionally paint *alla prima* (literally, "at the first," meaning a painting that is completed on one surface level, without overpainting), the vast majority of paintings require re-working, overpainting, changes and corrections. It takes three months for a normally thick first coat to dry enough for overpainting; by that time, most of the shrinkage of the paint will have occurred and another layer of oil may be applied without risking the later development of cracks in the surface. (How many artists today wait three months before reworking or overpainting a picture?) And the topmost layer must dry again for three to six months before a varnish may be applied. In the heavy painting of many moderns, a painting would require more than a year's lapse before varnishing may be safely done.

The problem of drying time with oils is further complicated by the varying degrees of wetness, or "fatness," in varying oil colors. Each pigment requires a different amount of vehicle because each has its own degree of absorption. Some colors contain up to 200 per cent oil in relation to pigment, and some as low as 20 per cent. Pigments such as Zinc White, Lead White, Cadmiums, and Opaque Chromium Green have a low oil content. Yellow Ochre, Raw Siena, Ultramarine Blue, and Titanium contain a medium amount of oil vehicle. Cobalt Blue, Burnt Siena, and Umbers have a moderately high oil content. Ivory Black, Prussian Blue, and Viridian are rich in oil. Alizarin, Phthalocyanines, and Lamp Black have a very high oil content.

This variation in oil content has resulted in a number of "rules" for creating oil paintings (rules which are not always followed by contemporary painters). Since paints contract when they dry, painting with oil paints must proceed from "lean" to "fat." That is, paints which contain very little oil vehicle (or those which have been thinned with turpentine or mineral spirits) should be applied to the canvas first. Over these go the paints which incorporate a larger amount of oil. If this process is reversed, the slow drying, fatty paints will be sealed under the fast drying, lean paints. When the fat paints underneath eventually dry, they will crack the surface of the already dry outside paints. (For the same reason, a painting should not be varnished until all contraction due to drying has taken place.)

The greatest boon that the synthetic paints give the artist (and especially the "action painter") is their fast drying time. Overpainting with polymer emulsions—which dry by the simple evaporation of water—may proceed within five minutes to two hours, depending on the type used and how it is applied. Even heavy impastos of an inch or more in thickness dry in less than ten hours. And, as we shall see, the synthetics do not present the problem of various drying times for various colors, and there is thus no need to paint from lean to fat. While the succeeding layers of paint in an oil painting remain as bonded layers, in a synthetic painting all paint forms one solid, flexible film of plastic as each new layer is applied. All layers expand and contract as a whole; cracks due to expansion and contraction are thus avoided.

Synthetic Resins. The essential ingredient in many synthetic paints is either of two synthetic resins (sometimes both): *acrylic* resins and *vinyl* resins. These synthetic resins are created by means of a chemical process known as "polymerization," which can dramatically change the appearance, the texture, and other characteristics of a substance. A "polymer" is formed by chemically uniting a number of like molecules, the basic chemical unit of any substance, into larger molecules, or units, thereby changing the physical properties of the substance without altering its essential composition. Thus, for example, a thin, volatile liquid "monomer" can be changed into a "polymer" that is a completely stable, non-volatile, tough and elastic solid.

Acrylic and vinyl resins have been used for a vast variety of purposes for about thirty years. Acrylics are the plastics produced under such familiar names as Plexiglas and Lucite, and are used to make dentures, clothing fabrics, house paints and automobile finishes,

Above left. THE ARTIST'S SON, TITUS, 31 1/8 × 23 1/4 inches, by Rembrandt, dated 1655. Medium: Oil. (Courtesy: The Metropolitan Museum of Art, Bequest of Benjamin Altman, 1913.)

Below left. THE LAUNDRESS, 19 1/2 × 13 inches, by Honore Daumier, Medium: Oil. (Courtesy: The Metropolitan Museum of Art, Bequest of Lizzie P. Bliss, 1931.)

These two paintings show the destruction and cracking to which most oil paintings are prone. Most of the paintings of the Old Masters show fine spider-web cracking or, as in the case of the Rembrandt, actual damage. More recent paintings, such as the Daumier, also exhibit this action (which is probably due as much to poor oil paints and disregard of oil painting techniques as to the normal deterioration of oils).

among a host of other products. A few of the vinyls' commercial uses are as adhesives, house paints, numerous hard plastic items, and in the treatment of textiles.

It is clear from this brief list that both the acrylics and the vinyls lend themselves to an almost incredible range of end products. And it is this adaptability to innumerable characteristics that permits the wide range of effects in synthetic paints. (Actually, the acrylic resins permit a greater choice of useful monomers to be used in formulation than do the vinyl resins, and therefore the acrylics are more widely used in synthetic paints today.) The addition of other ingredients broadens the varieties still more, so that today there are synthetic paints offering varying degrees of flexibility in handling, gloss and matte effects, thickness and thinness, etc., and all with different degrees of durability and elasticity.

Advantages as a Paint Medium. The properties achieved by acrylic resins and, to a lesser extent, vinyl resins which make them advantageous as a fine art medium are the following:

1. Great transparency. They do not impose a color of their own in the pigments with which they are mixed, and they do not yellow with age, as oil does.

2. High resistance to ultra violet light.

3. Excellent dispersion of pigment.

4. High elasticity, thus permitting maximum flexibility in paint films.

5. Fast drying.

6. They form a permanent protective film for the pigment, thus preserving the life of a painting.

7. Great adhesiveness to canvas or other painting supports (some synthetic media were originally developed as superior adhesives).

Synthetic Paint Tests. Numerous tests have proved that the synthetic media incorporate the qualities listed above. Specific testing information is given in *Appendices,* Part II.

One test has still to be accomplished: the test of time. The question remains in the minds of many whether an organic, chemically made composition will remain chemically stable for centuries. Although there is strong evidence that the compounds will remain stable, time alone will tell for sure. But that is the way oil proved itself, too—indeed, to a certain extent, *dis*proved itself—because even in the hands of the most meticulous Old Master, oil paintings have yellowed and suffered certain imperfections over the centuries. Microscopic examination of old paintings show that they are frequently covered with a fine network of minute cracks even when the paintings appear quite normal to the naked eye. These cracks caused by atmosphere and ultraviolet light will eventually allow the paintings to be attacked more severely and they will then flake and peel.

Many restorers today are using synthetics, with faith that they will prove the most durable means of repair even for oil paintings. The Monet painting *Blue Waterlilies* was badly charred and damaged by smoke in the 1958 fire at the New York Museum of Modern Art—except for several small areas which had been recently restored with a plastic-base paint. Jean Volkmer, Conservator of Painting at the museum, states that the museum now uses many synthetics in restoration processes. Holes are repaired with paper and synthetic emulsions, glazes are duplicated synthetically, and final synthetic varnishes applied. Volkmer says that good results are achieved so long as great care is taken to use the right synthetic for a particular purpose.

Orrin Riley of the Guggenheim Museum Department of Conservation says that both synthetic emulsions and solution resins have been used to repair paintings at the Guggenheim. Among the techniques used have been sprayed plastic glazes; a process in which plastic is painted on glass placed over the area to be restored—the plastic film is soaked off the glass and then applied directly to the painting with synthetic medium (in this manner painting can be exactly duplicated before the restored section is applied); tinfoil bound to a surface with plastic varnishes to achieve texture; cracked areas smoothed by attaching preshrunk, fine chiffon silk to the painting with synthetic varnish, with restoration proceeding over this.

Other museums and professional restorers have employed synthetics, too, especially with modern works in which heavy impastos begin to fall apart, or which contain numerous mixed media applications. Since the processes and media originally used are often unknown as well as faulty, the synthetics seem to be the only means to hold them together safely.

Varieties of Synthetic Media. The major portion of this book will discuss the varieties of synthetic paints on the market today. As we will see, some synthetic media can duplicate the appearance of such traditional media as oil and watercolor, and all can offer a paint quality of their own. Some media are commercially available already formulated and pigmented; others must be formulated and/or pigmented by the artist. Some media must be used with water, some with oil, and some with neither.

The acrylic resins and the vinyl resins can be used in a solution form—that is, dissolved in an appropriate liquid (Chapters 1 and 2, Part III, discuss their properties and handling characteristics). But by far the most popular, the most flexible and versatile of the synthetic media use the synthetic resins in an emulsion form. Part II of this book is devoted to these "Polymer Emulsions."

PART II
THE POLYMER EMULSIONS

Chapter 1 / Structure and Characteristics

An emulsion is the suspension of a very finely divided material in a liquid. A "polymer emulsion"—also known as "synthetic emulsion" or "polymer tempera"—is a synthetic emulsion created by suspending minute particles of synthetic resin in water. The water, as well as being the carrier to suspend the resin, provides the fluidity for the medium. If color pigments are suspended along with the resin in such an emulsion, a paint is formed. When the resultant polymer emulsion paint is applied, the water evaporates and the resin particles flow together to form a strong, coherent film of plastic which binds the pigment particles together.

There are three general types of polymer emulsion paints. Those with an *acrylic* resin base are most widespread in both manufacture and use. Those with a *polyvinyl acetate* base were used in the early stages of emulsion development. These polyvinyl acetate paints have largely been superseded by what are known as *copolymers*. Copolymer emulsions utilize a resin made by using two or more different kinds of basic chemicals in forming (or polymerizing) the resin. Acrylic resins are inherently highly flexible in most cases. To make polyvinyl acetate flexible enough for durability, various proportions of acrylic chemicals or other chemicals are incorporated in the formation of the resin polymer to form a copolymer.

The fact that water can be used as the emulsifying liquid for the synthetic resins is of key importance to the handling and drying properties of the polymer emulsions. None of the volatile thinners such as turpentine are used with the emulsions, either in manufacture or in painting. The manufacturer polymerizes the synthetic resin in water, the artist uses water as the only thinner, and all equipment such as brush and palette are cleaned with water. A polymer emulsion painting dries by the mere evaporation of water from the paint—a far faster process than the oxidation of oils. And, as soon as the water has evaporated the paint film has reached its final form of complete stability and insolubility.

When used correctly, the polymer emulsion paints offer greater versatility, control, speed in handling, brilliance, and durability than any other paint medium ever developed. Most of the commercial brands available today come in both matte and gloss media. The artist, by using these separately or in combination, can produce the precise degree of gloss and matte he desires. Impastos can be built up to any degree of thickness without endangering the life of a painting. The polymer emulsions can emulate oil, watercolor, tempera, casein and gouache, as well as create a rich range of effects of their own (Figure I).

They can also be used in bas-relief techniques, as a sculptural medium, and in printing processes.

The fact that the polymer emulsions can achieve the surface effects of other media such as oil and watercolor does not mean that they handle in the same way. The technical means of achieving a traditional effect with a synthetic medium are in fact usually far different from the ways the traditional media are used. Later chapters will discuss in detail the various techniques employed to achieve particular end results.

Pigmentation. The grinding of pigments into a polymer emulsion is not a simple matter of pouring in a bit of color and stirring. As with oil paints, each pigment requires a different amount of emulsion to produce a good paste with correct brushing qualities. For most colors, the same pigments are used in polymer emulsions as in oil paints. Some traditional pigments, however, such as Viridian and Alizarin Crimson, cannot be used in an acrylic emulsion because the acrylic, in its liquid form, is alkaline and will react with these synthetic pigments. Therefore, new synthetic pigments must be used in their stead. Some of the synthetic pigments, incidentally, have surpassed the traditional colors in permanency and stability.

Other chemicals, such as wetting

Figure 1. Various techniques possible with polymer paints.

A. Watercolor — Emulsion paints are thinned with water and applied with watercolor brushes. The bottom section was given a coat of clear water to achieve a wet-in-wet effect.

B. Casein — Direct from the jar or slightly thickened by water evaporation, the paints have the consistency of casein colors. Applications and manipulations are the same as with the traditional medium, with the exception that underlying areas, when dry, do not pick up.

C. Tempera — Thinned slightly with water, the emulsions handle as smoothly and flatly as do temperas. They dry matte. The upper line was done with a small watercolor brush; the bottom area, with a bristle brush.

D. Oil — Emulsion paints mixed with a gel medium immediately emulate oil paints. Their viscosity and body are very like those of oils, and the methods of application are similar. The emulsion paints dry faster, however. Large brush strokes hold their configuration. Scumbles, wet-in-wet, blendings, dry brush, and line are some of the techniques displayed here.

E. Impasto — Modeling paste is used with or without color for fast impasto. This area was handled completely with the palette knife.

F. Heavy Glazing — Gel medium and a small amount of color can create almost three-dimensional glazes, ranging from the transparent to the translucent.

G. Oil — A more brilliant and luminous oil

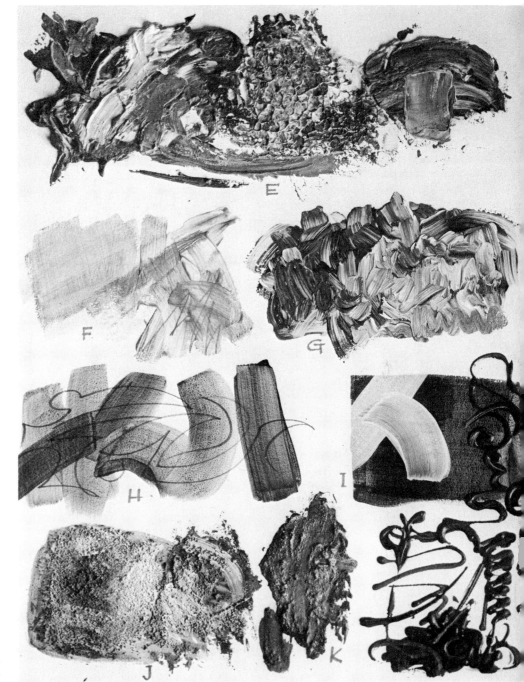

method is achieved by brushing on a film of clear gel medium and then painting directly into this with emulsion colors. The paints normally remain glossy but can be reduced to a semi-gloss by varnishing with a half-and-half mixture of matte varnish and gloss medium. Here the gel medium was applied in about a sixteenth-inch thickness with a palette knife. Small bristle brushes blended color into this.

H. Glazing—The lines were drawn under the glaze with a felt-point pen. Glazes were made by mixing gloss medium with a small amount of emulsion color; the more paint added, the less transparent the glaze. The texture of the illustration board upon which these demonstrations were done created the pebble texture under the glaze. When glazes are applied over smooth surfaces (such as gesso) the effect is as smooth as glass.

I. Translucent Multiple Glazes—A semi-opaque white glaze was applied over two layers of translucent paint. A much greater quantity of paint was added to the medium than in illustration H.

J. and K. Texture—The textures here were created by an admixture of sand (J) and powdered Fiberglas (K). The additives were first soaked with medium so they would not absorb binder from the paints with which they were mixed. Some scumbles of paint were applied over the dried surface.

L. Three-dimensional Line — Emulsion paint was mixed with gel medium and extruded from a plastic squeeze bottle of the cosmetic variety. The line remains flexible enough to be rolled on canvas and holds its impasto form.

agents, dispersing agents, preservatives, and thickeners, are added to polymer emulsions to stabilize the resin particles and pigments (that is, keep them in suspension) and to improve handling qualities and achieve good paint dispersion.

Drying Properties. As we have seen, polymer emulsion paints dry by the evaporation of water. As the water evaporates, the spheres of plastic resin approach and touch each other to form a paint film. The "viscosity" or "body" of water produced by added water soluble thickeners aids in holding the film of paint together so that this necessary final contact takes place. If the polymer emulsion is diluted too greatly with just water, the vehicle becomes so fluid that the resin spheres are spread too far apart to touch and form a film at the final stage of evaporation. That is, there is a certain minimum concentration of resin and of viscosity necessary to form a coherent paint film. Emulsions can only be thinned to a certain degree with water alone. Past that point some of the emulsion has to be added with the water to maintain minimum resin concentration.

All layers of polymer emulsion paints are compatible; that is, each layer of paint adheres with each succeeding layer to form one united surface which expands and contracts as a unit. Thus there is no danger of a lower layer cracking the surface layer, as there is

with oil paints, and the rules of oil painting—from "lean" to "fat"—do not apply. There is no change in the paint film after the water evaporates, no subsequent shrinking of the film, and no movement due to chemical aging as with oil paints. After the polymer emulsion dries, water will not affect it. In fact, soap and water are the recommended cleaning agents for polymer tempera paintings.

Toxicity. The *emulsion* forms of the synthetic paints are non-toxic and non-flammable. No toxic thinners are used in their production or in application. Other chemicals are incorporated in such minute quantities that they cannot harm the user. Ammonia, for example, which is a minor additive for some of the aqueous media, is in much lower concentration than in household cleansers.

Compatibility with Other Media. The synthetic emulsions will not mix with oils or solvents of any kind. To attempt this is to welcome disaster.

They will mix, however, with most water-based paints such as casein, tempera, color inks, and water colors, and with such special emulsion media as *Tri-Tec*. When polymer emulsions are added to such other paints, faster drying, greater resistance to water, and tougher films are achieved. Not all water paints, however, will work with polymer emulsions and every mixture should be tested for compatibility before one

goes ahead with painting.

Acrylic-base and vinyl-base polymer emulsions should not be mixed together. Acrylics are alkaline in nature while the vinyls are acidic, and reactions may occur. The two have been mixed at times for specific qualities desired by artists, but, generally, it should not be done.

Durability. When a polymer emulsion has dried into a paint film, it is unaffected by light, heat, or weather to an amazing extent. The painting will not crack, yellow, or darken with age so long as the basic rules of each medium and each brand, as recommended by the manufacturers, are followed.

Commercial acrylic resin emulsions have been used to paint numerous buildings in Florida and California. These paints have withstood the rigors of salt spray, high humidity, and a great amount of sun exposure, and they are still in good condition, some of them after ten years of service. A commercial oil paint would have failed in less than two years. The long life of these commercial grade polymer emulsions, which are not ground with the high quality pigment of an artist's paints, and probably contained some types of filler as well, testifies eloquently to the durability of the acrylic emulsions. The much higher standards set for a fine arts medium can only extend the life of a paint still further.

Chapter 2 / General Handling of Polymer Emulsions

It is possible for an artist to create his own polymer emulsion paints out of a synthetic resin emulsion, dry pigments, and the necessary chemicals—but it is not advisable. The various ratios of media to various pigments, the precise proportions of other additives, and the requirements of just the right amount of water in the paint are extremely sensitive matters which are best entrusted to reputable manufacturers with sound chemical backgrounds. The savings in money that might theoretically accrue in making one's own paints rarely happens in actuality, because there is considerable waste in individual formulations, and raw ingredients usually have to be bought in large bulk quantities. And the time and energy required in producing a single day's supply of paint is usually much better spent at the canvas.

Several prominent and reliable manufacturers produce polymer emulsions for the artist, and the list is growing every year as more and more artists switch from traditional to synthetic media. The brands based on acrylic resin are: *Liquitex*, manufactured by Permanent Pigments, Inc.; *Politec*, by Pinturas Plasticas, S.A., a Mexican firm; *Aqua-Tec*, by Bocour Artist Colors; *Shiva Acrylic*, by Shiva Artists Colors; and *Cryla*, by Rowney, an English company. Copolymer emulsion paints,

which use both acrylic and polyvinyl resins in their makeup, are *New Masters*, by California Products Corp. and *Hyplar*, by M. Grumbacher Co. The only synthetic emulsion that used vinyl resin alone was called simply *Polymer Tempera*. This is no longer on the market, but its inventor, Alfred Duca, has released the formula to the public for the benefit of those artists who wish to produce their own *Polymer Tempera* paints.

There are a few other brands of polymer emulsion available, but some of these are so new at this writing that artists have not had time to complete a painting with them, and in the case of some others, the manufacturers have made available so little information about them that they must be omitted from this book. Other large manufacturers of artists' materials have indicated that they plan to enter the plastic paints industry in the near future.

Liquitex was one of the first acrylic emulsions to appear on the market. Because it has been used for almost a decade by professional artists, its qualities are better known than those of more recent brands, and therefore *Liquitex* comprises the bulk of illustrative material in this book. But the handling techniques described in relation to these illustrations would

apply equally well to the other acrylic-base lines, and the differences that arise with the vinyls and copolymers are not major.

Consistency. Polymer emulsion paint brands are available in two varieties: those packaged in *tubes*, which have a thick body similar to that of oil paints, and those packaged in *jars*, which have a consistency somewhat between that of casein and tempera.

Tube colors can be used directly for heavy brushings and knife pilings, as they hold very sharp brush and knife configurations. Tube colors should be used when the artist wants duplication of oil painting techniques without the intermediary steps of building a more viscous body with additives or mediums which is necessary with jar colors. The tube colors handle and "feel" the same as tubed oil paints. Tube colors are also more convenient to store and carry.

Tube colors dry more slowly than jar colors and can be placed onto a palette for mixing and working in the usual oil method. If kept in small piles on the palette they are workable for a full day. If brushed out thinly or diluted with water they dry in about fifteen to thirty minutes. If a skin forms over the paint on the palette it can be lifted off and the paint underneath will still be

1

2

Color Plate 1. WOMAN 23, 24×48 inches, by Russell Woody, 1962. Medium: *Liquitex.*

This is an *alla prima* painting which was painted directly on a Masonite panel with no ground or underpainting. Paints were mixed with modeling paste and gloss medium. Consistency ranged from that of a buttery paste to a very viscous, putty-like mixture. Large bristle brushes were used in most areas. The whole painting was kept wet and workable from start to finish. Wet paint was applied over wet paint, allowed to stand, or blended in. When the impasto areas began to set, final, but limited, overpainting completed the work.

Color Plate 2. PREGNANT WOMAN, 48×30 inches, by Russell Woody, 1961. Medium: *Liquitex.*

The texture of this painting was created with modeling paste, heavily applied with a palette knife. When the paste was partially dry on the panel, it was incised with the end of a brush. Semi-dry portions of paste caused the lumps of texture. Lines were drawn with the palette knife. Approximately twenty glazes were thinly brushed over the textured areas. They range from the transparent to the almost opaque.

The support used was an eighth-of-an-inch Masonite panel. The underpainting was in blue with black over-glazes.

soft enough to use if it has not dried overnight.

Tube colors can be diluted with half water, half polymer medium (see below) to achieve jar color body and any of the manipulations characteristic of jar colors.

Jar colors are not as thick and buttery as oil paints. If this viscous quality is desired, the paints can be thickened somewhat by placing the caps on the jars upside down and letting the water evaporate slightly. A better method is to use gel medium (see below) which gives the paint handling qualities comparable to oil. Aggregates such as Celite or marble dust can be added to achieve this objective, and a modeling paste may also be used with moderation. (Demonstrations F, J and K in Figure 1 show some effects with various additives.)

Very little separation of pigment from medium occurs with a well formulated polymer emulsion, but if a milky liquid should appear on top of the jar colors, it is merely the emulsion binder and should be stirred in. The glass jars give the artist wide-mouthed containers into which he can dip the brush directly. Since jar color dries very quickly, it is better to work in this manner than to arrange colors on the palette. If too much paint is placed on the palette, a good portion of it will be wasted, since the polymer emulsions do not redissolve when dry.

Polymer emulsion paints dry much more slowly in glass or plastic jars, even with the caps off, than they do on the palette. This is because less surface is exposed to air and therefore less evaporation of water occurs. If polymer emulsions do begin to dry in the containers they dry from the top down. A skin forms on the surface. The artist need only reach into the jar and lift off this skin, and the rest of the paint is in perfect condition. Some painters place a few drops of water on top of the colors to prevent drying, but this is not recommended because it dilutes the paint too much. When colors become very thick however, a little water should be stirred in. Even these minor problems of drying never occur when caps are replaced after each use.

The rims of jars must be wiped after use or the paint will dry on the rims and

make removal of the tops very difficult. Skins forming on the rims or sides of the containers should also be removed before they become incorporated with the paint. Although I am a very sloppy painter at times and am lax in following the above rules, I seldom have any trouble with tight caps or skinning. If a jar top does become hard to remove, a wide jar top remover or pliers easily overcomes the problem. An easier method is to run hot water over the lid for a few minutes, and it will come off with no trouble.

Thinning. Polymer emulsions cannot be mixed with oil paints or other mediums or varnishes that have other than a water base (with the exceptions that will be noted below). Thinners such as turpentine or mineral spirits must not be mixed with emulsion colors or mediums.

Both polymer emulsion jar and tube colors may be thinned with water if the artist wishes to increase the flow or transparency of the paint. But thinning should be done only to a limited degree. Too much water will produce too great mobility and the paint will lack the cohesion necessary for control. There is also the danger of leaching or washing out the binder necessary to hold the particles together. Whenever any great extent of thinning is done, one of the polymer mediums should be added along with the water.

Drying. When used in a pure state direct from the jar, and under normal studio conditions of humidity and temperature, polymer emulsion paints dry within ten to fifteen minutes after application. If the paint is mixed with polymer medium or varnish, the drying time is increased to about fifteen to twenty minutes. Heavy impasto applications take from one to eight hours to reach surface hardness, depending on the thickness and how long the paint is worked. Tube colors dry within about thirty minutes in normal applications, and if painting does not continue over the wet color.

The polymer emulsions can be painted over as soon as they become dry to the touch, or worked in an *alla prima* technique. This is true even in thick applications.

Figure 2. The palette for synthetic emulsions.

A slab of white opaque glass makes the best palette for the synthetic paints. The opaque glass shown here is a section of the variety that is used to decorate the fronts of buildings. Almost every kind of paint mentioned in this book—including oils, temperas, caseins, and watercolors, as well as synthetics—has been mixed on it.

Buckets of water are arranged on both sides of the glass palette. (I use eight such buckets.) Brushes must not be allowed to dry when they contain the synthetic emulsions, so each is immediately dropped into a bucket after use. The brush is agitated in one bucket after another, and by the time it reaches the last bucket, it is thoroughly clean and can be wiped, shaped, and returned to a brush container. No scrubbing or scraping is necessary.

Since water is the only cleansing agent necessary for brushes as well as palette, the clean-up procedure with synthetic media is about as simple and unmessy as possible.

Most polymer emulsion colors dry relatively matte, and brilliancy seems to diminish upon drying. This brilliancy is restored when a gloss polymer medium (see next paragraph) is brushed over the colors. The artist should thus not become alarmed when a vibrant passage seems to lose its quality upon drying, since the wet color effects return with an overlay of medium. The artist adjusts to this factor quickly; after several paintings, his mind almost automatically makes the necessary compensations as to terminal results.

Generally, tube colors dry to a slight sheen while jar colors dry very flat.

Gloss and Matte Media. The polymer lines usually include two kinds of colorless media, one a gloss and the other a matte, which may be mixed with the paints in a wide range of dilutions to give any desired degree of gloss or matte to the colors. The gloss medium, sometimes called "polymer medium," produces a moderately glossy effect when mixed with paints. If more than one-quarter medium to three-quarters color is used, the colors tend to become transparent. If maximum opacity is desired as well as gloss, the paints should be applied directly from the jar or tube with no dilution and a coat of polymer medium brushed over the painting when it is dry (see *Final Varnishes* below).

Matte medium, which gives a matte tone, can also be mixed with the colors in any proportion, depending on the degree of transparency desired. Unlike gloss medium, however, matte medium should not be used as a final varnish, because its colloidal silica content in some lines may produce a chalky glaze over dark colors. If a matte varnish is included in the line of the particular paint brand used, this should be employed for final varnishing.

My painting *Seated Woman: Sixth to Ninth Hour* (Figure 3) is conceived in terms of contrast between matte and gloss surfaces.

Final Varnishes. A polymer emulsion painting can be washed with water and does not necessarily require a final varnish. However, to provide a protective surface which would absorb physical wear, to protect thin glazes and watered down paints, or to adjust the degree of surface gloss or matte to a desired level, a varnish may be applied in either a gloss or matte finish. Polymer medium, as we have seen, can be used to achieve the gloss varnish effect. For a matte effect, matte varnish should be used. This specially formulated matte varnish contains hard wax and little colloidal silica. It gives a satiny non-glare surface from which reflection is prevented to an amazing extent.

Varnishing of a polymer painting may proceed as soon as the paint is dry. A small amount of water may be added to the varnish to facilitate a more even flow, but it should not be made too thin. Varnish should be applied with a wide, soft hair brush of good quality. The brush should be relatively thin so that too much varnish will not be deposited.

To achieve an even coat, varnishing should be accomplished as rapidly and smoothly as possible in continuous strokes from one side of the painting to the other, either vertically or horizontally, as the artist prefers. Overexuberant brush work, however, will produce a froth of bubbles. If bubbles do occur, a completely dry brush should be quickly wiped over the affected area before it dries, and the bubbles will disappear.

Varnish should not be restroked over partially dried varnish or the film will rub up in flake-like particles which become bound in the painting. If it is necessary to apply a second coat of varnish, this should not be done until the first coat is completely dry. If the matte finish is desired, it is good practice to first varnish with a gloss polymer medium and, after that has dried, to apply a coat of matte varnish.

On large paintings, a relatively small area should be varnished, allowed to dry, and then another area varnished. Since a small wet area can be corrected or wiped off easily this will allow for any corrections to be made before drying takes place. If an area is inadvertently skipped, it can be varnished after the first coat is dry. Overlapping of brush strokes is not detectable because of the leveling qualities of the varnishes.

The varnishes look milky when immediately applied over a painting, but they dry clear as glass within a few

Figure 3. SEATED WOMAN: SIXTH TO NINTH HOUR, 26×21 inches, by Russell Woody, 1963. Medium: *Liquitex*.

The key to this painting, which is almost entirely black except for parts of the central figure, is the interplay between matte and high gloss. Modeling paste mixed with black paint was heavily applied with the brush to the area at the top. The lower half is a flat black. In the illustration the top looks gray in relation to the lower half. The two areas are of the same black intensity, however; the contrast between the two is seen because the top is a high gloss while the bottom is completely matte.

Yellow Oxide and Siena glazes were employed in underpainting the figure and show through. An intense yellow outlines the area at the right. The rest is black and white. The figure itself as well as the entire upper area of the painting were given two coats of gloss medium to increase the gloss and the contrast with the lower area. The bottom black was varnished with matte varnish.

minutes, and create a brilliantly transparent film which will never yellow or change color.

A special varnish technique used by Syd Solomon may be of interest to other artists. Solomon, who has worked with synthetics for years, mixes his own varnish for paintings. He shaves beeswax into a double boiler, melts it, pours polymer medium into it, and warms the mixture. The proportion of wax to medium is varied according to the degree of gloss desired; the more wax

the less gloss. To varnish a painting he blows the warm mixture through a mouth atomizer onto the painting. He always varnishes outdoors on sunny days, because a sun-warmed painting seems to reduce the pull of the varnish against the paint and also helps avoid bubbles. Sometimes he uses a cheap Flit gun instead of a mouth atomizer; if so, he throws the gun away after use because it becomes clogged with dry varnish.

If an artist prefers the spray technique to the brush, the varnish should be thinned with water from 20 to 40 per cent. A mixture should be allowed to stand if air bubbles are present. The best method of spraying is to use a high quality, high pressure spray gun which delivers a fan type spray action. An excellent small spray unit is Sprayon Jet-Pak manufactured by Sprayon Products, Inc., of Cleveland, Ohio. Pressure is delivered from a non-toxic, non-flammable pressure can attached to a sprayer head. It is inexpensive and gives a perfect spray mist for polymers. If this cannot be obtained, a Flit gun or mouth atomizer can be used. Care must be taken that large globules of varnish are not sprayed onto the painting; test the action of the spray on another surface before proceeding. Too much spray will run or puddle on the surface. To prevent this, a quick back and forth motion should be used until a very thin, even coat of varnish is applied.

Fixative. Matte varnishes make an excellent fixative for all types of graphic media such as pastel, conté, or chalk. The matte varnish should be thinned with water so it will spray easily from the particular atomizer or sprayer used (see above). Usually a mixture of about half water and half medium will work. When a gloss medium is used it will heighten the colors and make them more brilliant, as well as give a gloss appearance. Either type of medium will make work done in poster colors, temperas, caseins, watercolors, and soluble inks insoluble and water proof. Care must be taken in spraying that the water mediums do not run. Several fine sprays are much better than one heavy spray.

Gel Medium. A few companies manufacture a thick gel medium which can be mixed with polymer emulsion jar colors to give them a viscosity similar to that of oil media. This gel is a pure polymer emulsion and is of the same milky color as a gloss polymer medium or matte medium; as it comes from the jar it looks like cold cream. But like the other media, it dries clear and colorless. (See Chapter 4 for a discussion of how to use gel medium in painting. Also, see Figure 1 – F, G and L.)

Modeling Paste. Most polymer emulsion lines include a modeling paste, sometimes labeled "modeling paste and extender." The modeling paste is a very stiff, white or cream colored putty made by adding marble dust to the polymer medium. It may be used to build three-dimensional forms and to produce impasto, over which polymer emulsion colors are glazed or painted.

The marble dust addition reduces the flexibility of the medium to the point that modeling paste should not be used on canvas in any substantial degree of thickness, or it is liable to crack. Rigid supports should be used. However, if gel medium is mixed with paste in the ratio of one to one or two to one, the paste becomes flexible enough to use on canvas. If cracking should occur, spraying with water from an atomizer will alleviate the condition.

Modeling paste may be mixed with paints in order to make them go further. While this is excellent for student purposes, extenders should not be mixed with paints for serious work. When modeling paste is mixed with colors, sufficient medium should also be added to give the paint flexibility. The amount of medium depends on the support upon which it is to be applied; more medium is needed for flexible supports than for rigid ones.

Single layers of modeling paste as it comes from the can should be no more than one-quarter inch thick. If piled on heavily the paste tends to dry too fast and crack. If a greater thickness is desired, succeeding layers can be added, to achieve depths of up to two inches and more.

Other purposes to which modeling paste lends itself are frame decorating, printing techniques, sculpture, bas relief, and restoration of three-dimensional objects of stone, wood, plaster and the like.

Color Plates 1 and 2 (page 22) illustrate various effects that can be achieved with the use of modeling paste.

Gesso. A synthetic gesso is available in all of the polymer emulsion brands. This ready-to-use liquid ground material has proved to be one of the fastest selling items to hit the art market in years. The synthetic gessos may be used as grounds not only for the emulsion paints, but are excellent for use with oils, watercolors, tempera, and encaustic, and they even make ideal surfaces for silverpoint drawing. They protect canvas fibers and any other commonly used support. And they dry immediately, thus eliminating the waiting time after preparing traditional grounds.

Traditional gesso is basically chalk or some other inert white material bound with a gelatin or casein glue. It is not flexible and should not be used on flexible supports. The synthetic gessos, in contrast, have a synthetic emulsion base and are thus pliable enough to use as a ground for canvas, and permit the canvas to be rolled when a painting is completed.

Synthetic gesso may be applied in one or more coats depending on the surface quality desired. It can be sprayed or brushed on. An excellent tooth is obtained by using a felt roller (commonly used with aqueous house paints) to roll on the gesso in two to three coats. Rolling should continue until the desired tooth is obtained, and then immediately stopped so the gesso can dry. A very even, smooth coating is achieved when gesso is diluted with about fifteen to thirty per cent water and brushed on in three or more applications. In brushing gesso, each coat should be applied at right angles to the preceding one so that brush marks are minimized. For toned ground, the gesso may be tinted with the polymer emulsion colors.

Many types of textural effects can be accomplished by incorporating inert additives with the gesso. Grounds of this sort should be used on rigid panels. Sand, marble dust, Celite, fiber glass particles, and modeling paste are a few of the materials that may be added. Each additive should be completely soaked in the gesso before application. If the mixtures become too dry or pasty, a polymer medium should be used to replace whatever medium is soaked up by the textural particles.

The intense whiteness of the synthetic gessos does not discolor with age, and it enhances the brilliance of transparent colors or glazes. Since the reflective and refractive index of the synthetics is greater than that of traditional media, a white ground produces a more brilliant and intense color under transparent pigments and glazes even when traditional media are used.

Painting Supports. The synthetic emulsions will adhere to any surface that is not oily or greasy or which does not have an impervious, non-porous surface such as glass or metal. The range of possible supports is thus almost limitless. Following is a list of supports which have been used for a variety of qualities and effects:

Canvas of all types (raw canvas is best); burlap; linen; cotton; cheese cloth applied to board; synthetic fabrics such as Orlon; sailcloth; Masonite, hardboard, fiberboard, and the like; wood; paper of all types including rice paper, tissue paper, toweling, and Kraft paper; chipboard, matboard, illustration board, cardboard and the like; masonry surfaces of all types.

The average oil-primed canvas manufactured for the artist has a sufficiently low quantity of oil that the water-base paints can form a bond to them, but they are not highly recommended. Raw canvas is the best cloth support, though the backs of oil-primed canvas will also serve. Some companies are now producing polymer-primed canvas coated with a polymer gesso specially suitable for synthetic painting.

Synthetic paints actually protect the cloth surfaces upon which they are used, as opposed to the deteriorative effects caused by oils. Thus, a sizing is not necessary, as it is with oil paints in order that the medium may not attack and destroy the support. Grounds, such as polymer gesso, may be used with synthetics, in order to gain a special surface quality or to seal porus supports. Highly porous or absorbent surfaces should be given a prime so the water will not be removed from the succeeding layers of emulsion so fast that coherent films do not form.

Since the synthetics protect the support, less expensive materials can be used—a fact which makes the synthetics especially desirable to the student.

A canvas painted with an average thickness of polymer paint can be rolled up as soon as the paint is dry; sometimes within ten minutes after the final brush stroke has been laid. The polymer emulsions produce the most flexible paint

film available today. For transportation and storage purposes this quality is very advantageous.

When heavy impasto is applied, and especially if aggregates are used to a great extent, a more rigid support is needed because of a decrease in flexibility of the entire paint film. Masonite is probably the best rigid surface to work upon. The untempered kind is preferred. Tempered Masonite, though stronger, has a treated, shiny surface which should be sanded before applying a polymer tempera in order to gain a better bond between support and medium. The resulting dust can be saved and mixed with the paint to give a finely textured ground.

Polymer emulsions should not be painted over oil paints unless and until the oils have completely dried and lost their shine or slick oil surface. Conversely, the emulsions make excellent grounds and underpainting for oils. They protect the canvas, and oils will readily adhere to them.

If very lightweight or highly flexible or fragile materials are desired as a support, these can be attached to a rigid or semi-rigid backing by using the polymer temperas as glue.

The acrylic emulsions lend themselves especially well to mural painting on masonry surfaces. The paints do not sink into a porous material but remain on its surface. In addition, the acrylics are an alkaline emulsion and therefore resistant to alkali. Thus they will not react with masonry supports of alkali content and can even be applied over plaster, mortar and cement before they have fully aged.

This brief list of support types only begins to suggest the diverse possibilities with polymer emulsion paints, and further details will be given in later chapters dealing with specific techniques. If the artist wishes to test a new kind of support, he should paint a layer of emulsion on the surface and, when it is dry, wet the surface thoroughly with water. If the emulsion does not peel up when rubbed, it will remain on the support indefinitely.

The Palette. Since the polymer emulsions do not adhere to smooth and shiny surfaces (other than those produced by the media themselves), the best palette

is one which has this kind of surface. Glass is most useful (Figure 2). When the aqueous media dry on the glass, they can be brushed with water and the paint will literally float to the top of the thin film of water. The skins of plastic can then be scraped off with the palette knife if portions still adhere, or wiped off with a rag. The whole process of cleaning the palette will take less than two minutes, and no thinners or removers are needed—only water.

An opaque white glass of one-quarter inch thickness is best. Its whiteness allows the artist to mix on the glass and see the true tones and tints he is to use on the painting. If opaque glass is not obtainable, a clear glass with a sheet of white paper underneath will be an excellent substitute. The paper must be firmly attached so that water and paint will not run under the glass and discolor the paper. This can be done by using plastic tape entirely around the paper, sticking it to the edges of the glass.

Another good palette is one of white porcelain known as a butcher's tray. These are often sold in art supply shops for watercolor palettes. A sheet of Plexiglas or Lucite will also serve as a palette. Masonite can be used, but it cannot be cleaned as easily as the glass or glassy types. The paper palettes manufactured for use with oil paints will serve in some cases—though these are somewhat less than satisfactory even for oils. They stick together if the paint runs, and they buckle when used with aqueous media.

A container palette which will keep color moist for a long period can be fashioned from plastic ice trays or egg trays and covered with foil or self sealing plastic wrapping.

Polymer emulsions dry as fast on the palette as on the painting; from five to ten minutes in films and from ten to thirty minutes in mass. Paint should not be allowed to dry on the palette, nor should other colors be mixed over those that are dry. The dry colors will float up when wet by new paint, and skins will mix into the fresh colors, ruining them. Since the palette is so quickly and easily cleaned, it is not much trouble to keep it free of old paint mixtures.

Despite the advisability of working as much as possible from covered containers, polymer emulsion colors can be mixed on a glass palette at the time of use, or, if a large area is to be painted, the colors can be mixed on the palette and then stored in covered jars (and a palette is indeed required with the use of polymer emulsion tube colors).

Brushes. Any type of artist's brush, watercolor as well as oil, may be used with polymer emulsions. The medium is, however, somewhat harsh on fine sables, and I have found that many cheap house painting brushes with nylon bristles perform more satisfactorily. Sometimes I cut these to particular shapes I find useful, and I am happier cutting a sixty-cent brush than a five-dollar one. After using hundreds of makes, models, and kinds, I prefer to paint with brushes made by the Harrison Brush Co., or Robert Simmons Co., or with low cost house painting brushes made of nylon. They are especially desirable in the larger sizes. When soaked in water over long periods of time, their extra-long ferrules do not split, nor does the paint on the handles crack. The common household brushes cost less and actually perform better than the cheaper varieties of brushes manufactured for artists' use. One excellent and inexpensive brush, however, is the art utility brush supplied for school use by the J. L. Hammett Co.

Cleaning. After a polymer emulsion painting dries, water will no longer affect it. Thus, soap and water are the recommended cleaning agents.

Some artists attach information sheets to the backs of all polymer emulsion paintings, stating the type of synthetic, its characteristics, and cleaning procedures. All synthetic paintings should carry a notation of this kind so that cleaning will not be done with solvents, and so that, in case of damage, proper restoration will be made.

Artist Raymond Jonson's information sheet reads, in part: "When cleaning becomes necessary, use suds made with a pure soap and lukewarm distilled water. Here are three different means for cleaning, depending on condition of the paint surface and degree of dirt; a one-and-one-half-inch wide soft bristle brush for careful scrubbing;

an elephant ear sponge which is fine grained and soft; absorbent cotton wads. Several rinsings are necessary to make certain that all soap is removed. Do not allow water to remain on the surface longer than necessary.

"Organic solvents and other cleaners used in cleaning oil paintings should not be used on polymers because they would ruin them. Never use any abrasives as they can mar the surface, and never apply varnishes intended for oil paintings as they can damage the work.

"With few exceptions, surfaces of polymer must not be put against any other materials, especially under pressure. The polymer has a tendency to act as a contact adhesive, and particularly so if placed against another surface of polymer or of glass. If surfaces of dry polymer paint are put against one another under pressure they could become permanently welded together. If glass is used to cover a painting, there must be adequate space between it and the surface of the work so they cannot press against one another.

"The foregoing may seem to indicate that this polymer paint is inferior to oil paint. It is not and, in certain respects, is superior. It should never crack for it is flexible. Being free from oils and their varnishes, it cannot change in value or color due to them."

The advice is excellent.

Although cleaning with soap and water is best, I have used household abrasive cleaners in certain stubborn cases when grease and dirt from hands have soiled a work.

Artist Barclay Sheaks also glues an informative note to the backs of his paintings, which reads: "This painting is done in acrylic polymer and under normal conditions should need little or no care over several lifetimes except for occasional wipings with a damp cloth. Acrylic polymer is a plastic medium which has a durability and resistance to wear, dust, dirt, smoke, smog, and time which surpasses that of other mediums, including oil paint. It contains no varnish, or oil, or resins, or gums to crack, turn yellow or deteriorate. When finished, this painting can be compared to a solid plastic sheet of Plexiglas.

"Should this painting become soiled or dirty, it needs only to be cleaned with warm, mild soapy water. Since it contains no varnishes, it has none to remove or restore. THEREFORE DO NOT USE HARSH SOLVENTS SUCH AS LACQUER THINNER, ACETONE, VOLATILE SPIRITS. THESE CAN DAMAGE THE PAINTING."

Cost. Most polymer emulsion colors and mediums are much cheaper than oil paints. The two-ounce size, for example, is generally priced from fifty cents to $1.35, depending on the color. Because the synthetic medium both brushes more easily and makes more efficient use of the pigment than does oil, the two-ounce bottle or tube is equivalent to almost two studio size tubes of oil color. It can easily be seen that economy is not the least outstanding feature of using synthetic emulsions.

But low original cost is not the only means of achieving economy with synthetic emulsions. Because the aqueous synthetics protect the supports on which they are used, cheaper supports can be used than with traditional media. Oil paints, for example, tend to rot canvas, and expensive types of treated canvas should be used, and a protective ground applied in order to preserve the painting. But the synthetic emulsions can be used with low-grade canvas, and no grounds need be applied before painting begins.

The synthetics adhere to a vast variety of supports, as detailed earlier, and an economy-minded artist can select the very cheapest with confidence. Some of my students have used very cheap papers in experimental painting with synthetic emulsions. Whenever one of these paintings was deemed of such a quality that it should be saved, the painting was varnished by the student and backed to Masonite or canvas, using polymer medium as a glue. This medium is not only superior to most glues produced, it also protects the materials. The painting thus has as great durability as one executed on the highest quality canvas.

Another reduction in cost results from the use of water as a cleaning agent rather than turpentine or other thinners and solvents.

Chapter 3 / Polymer Emulsion Used for its Own Characteristics

Polymer emulsion brands of paint possess certain native characteristics in appearance and handling that are different from all other media. These characteristics have not been exploited by artists to any great degree as yet, but interest is growing. As Syd Solomon says, "The culmination of new media application will come when artists begin to use the synthetics for their own properties of technical expression." And James Brooks agrees: "It will be interesting to see what happens when artists start to use the emulsions as a water medium (rather than a substitute for oils) and explore its true character."

All acrylic- and vinyl-base polymer emulsion paints have a heightened brilliance of color. The pigments are absolutely pure to the eye, their hues totally unaffected by the medium (as soon as the paints are dry). This brilliance is due to the complete transparency of the acrylic resin binder. The transparency of the resin gives another quality, too: a quality of light reflection and refraction within the paints that provides a luminosity and a sense of depth unattainable in any other medium. The colors seem to glow from within.

This quality of transparency can be employed to extremely subtle effects in painting. With oil paints, color nuances are often achieved by blending and mixing colors on the canvas. The polymer emulsions dry too fast to permit this, except in their relatively new tube form. However, a new kind of color fusion can be attained by a succession of thin glazes. The eye penetrates the various films to experience new color sensations. For glazing, any proportion of polymer emulsion color with either type of medium (gloss or matte varnish) may be used; the lower the proportion of color in the mixture, the greater number of glaze coats that can be built up to develop the color desired and to produce a greater depth of films for accentuated light reflection. Succeeding layers of glaze should not be applied until the previous layer has dried, which is only a matter of minutes. Artists have only begun to experiment with this new method of glazing.

For a very thin glaze, the paint may be rubbed on with the fingers or thumb, as the Old Masters did with oils. This technique should be accomplished quickly, because of the paint's rapid drying. Glazes, of any paint, are somewhat delicate. A varnish of a clear polymer medium should be applied to protect them from damage.

The major complaint that artists trained in traditional oil methods have against the polymer emulsions is that they dry too fast. Surely this characteristic can be turned to an advantage, and I personally consider it to be one.

Fast drying allows for immediate expression, and it trains the artist to be sure of hand and exact in intent. A painting can be altered or corrected, or it can yield to slow and thoughtful development, by means of simple overpainting—a process much less disenchanting than the messy and time consuming mechanics of scraping off wet, muddy paint. Glazes and impastos can proceed to completion in days, while the artist is still "in the mood" of a certain painting, instead of waiting for months to resume work on a painting which has finally dried sufficiently to permit overpainting.

The jar colors, when used without gel medium or modeling paste, are thinner in quality than oils, they do not have the pull or the drag, and they do not reveal brush strokes nearly so much. These qualities need not be considered inherent drawbacks, but merely a different set of characteristics that can be exploited to different results. The tube colors readily give oil-like painting characteristics when used directly from the tube. Many artists feel that synthetics do not achieve the air of "importance" or the "presence" that oil paintings have. But surely this is merely an emotional reaction, without reasonable basis. The chief reason that oil paintings have come to be regarded as *the* important medium is the durabi-

29

lity and color accuracy that could be achieved with oils: painters could paint "for eternity"—or at least posterity. It will be a real breakthrough when we finally overcome our staid habits of mind in regard to oil and realize that synthetics have all of the advantages and none of the drawbacks of oil.

James Brooks, the well-known abstractionist, is one artist who has become enthusiastic about the possibilities of the synthetics in their own right. He began working with synthetics as an answer to problems in mural paintings in the 1930's, and has experimented with various kinds ever since. Some of his earlier experiments proved unsuccessful, from a durability standpoint, because he made the mistake of mixing oil with synthetic resins, or used oils over emulsions in finishing a painting. Today most of his paintings are executed completely with aqueous synthetics.

Brooks' usual technique today, as shown in *Blokkop* (Figure 4) and *Cooba* (Figure 5), is to first apply a ground of Dutch Boy Latex White, which gives a pure white base for the luminous colors, and then paint with acrylic colors in a way that exploits their inherent properties. "The eye," he says, "may be sensitive to one one-hundredth of an inch difference in the depth of paint surface, and therefore should react to the quality of depth presented by each medium." He builds up a painting with combinations of thin washes and opaque paints. He rubs on thin tints and tones of color with a rag or paper. Areas of liquid paint are applied and then blotted off with an absorbent paper. If more viscous paint is desired for a textural effect in certain passages, he adds asbestine to the colors as an extender (asbestine tints the color slightly, but not appreciably). The painting gradually builds, and when completed it has a depth and luminosity and a translucent quality that are the very touchstones of the polymer emulsions. (These qualities regrettably are not too apparent in black and white reproduction.)

Elaine de Kooning also prefers to let the qualities of the acrylic emulsions be seen. She was introduced to *Liquitex* by Raymond Jonson when she was in New Mexico in 1958 as a visiting professor at the state university. Every weekend while there she would go to Juarez,

Mexico, to see the *corridas*, where she made many sketches which she later turned into a series of bullfight paintings. The piercing immediacy and brightness of polymer emulsion paints were ideal for her objective of capturing the brilliance of the colors of Mexico and sensuous excitement of the bullfight. The fast drying of the medium also contributed to the rather passionate paintings.

In creating these paintings (*Juarez: Charging Bull*, Color Plate 3, opposite, is a good example), Elaine de Kooning usually used the emulsion straight from the jar. Some color-blending was done on the painting, with water or polymer medium sometimes used. The agitated action of the paintings was created through overlapping and juxtaposed contours. In our example, the splayed banderillas stuck into the bull served as the basis of the composition. In some of Miss de Kooning's bullfight paintings, acrylic emulsion paints were used as an underpainting and the final surface done in oils.

Elaine de Kooning sometimes uses canvas as a support for polymer paintings, but she usually favors Masonite panels backed with one-inch by three-inch wood strips along its edges. She applies a coat of gesso or Titanium White as a ground.

Miss de Kooning's sudden shifts of paint, and sense of action produced by emphasized contours, can be seen in the portrait of Caryl Chessman (Figure 6). This was done on watercolor paper with a gesso covering. The gesso provides a semi-absorbent ground and a slight pull and tooth on which to work. The only pigments used were black and white, to which some paste was added to give body. (Miss de Kooning, incidentally, has had a complete show of black and white polymer paintings.) The artist's deep emotional involvement can easily be felt in the portrait, which was done from composite photographs. (Miss de Kooning organized a protest march in New York City against Chessman's death penalty, and sent over $450 worth of telegrams expressing her objections to California Governor Brown and to newspapers.)

A technique Miss de Kooning considers one of the outstanding features of the polymer emulsions was used in this

Color Plate 3. JUAREZ: CHARGING BULL, ca. 4 feet high, by Elaine de Kooning, 1959. Medium: *Liquitex*. (Courtesy: the artist.)

Juarez: Charging Bull is one of a series of *corrida* paintings in which Elaine de Kooning uses the emulsion colors for their brilliance and color strength to reflect the sport's intensity as well as its color. Banderillas stuck into the bull suggested the basis for the abstract construction.

Miss de Kooning used Masonite, braced on the back with one-by-three-inch stripping. She brushed the panel with two coats of *Liquitex* Gesso for a ground. Her painting was direct and was accomplished in three sessions. Her colors were mostly mixed together with water and/or polymer medium on a glass palette, although she also did some mixing directly on the painting with colors from the jars. The heavy strokes and brush marks were achieved by adding modeling paste to the paints. The white ground was often reestablished by painting out.

Finally, two coats of polymer medium were applied as a varnish.

Color Plate 4. TEMPLATE, 74×42 inches, by Milton Resnick, 1960. Medium: *Liquitex*. (Courtesy: Howard Wise Gallery, New York.)

That polymer emulsions do not have to be used for brilliant color is illustrated by this painting by Milton Resnick. Resnick seems almost to reduce or subdue color intensity with his pigment combinations. Here *Liquitex* was applied directly on a large sheet of paper. The colors were mixed, but there was not much overpainting. Resnick uses very little paint but nonetheless achieves a heavily overpainted effect. The result is an appearance of great depth and projection. Many of Resnick's paintings are listed and sold as oils; it is difficult to tell the difference.

This large painting on paper is backed to canvas, stretched and framed in the normal fashion.

Color Plate 5. BLUE CAUSEWAY, 57×72¾ inches, by Helen Frankenthaler, 1963. Medium: *Aqua-Tec*. (Courtesy: the artist.)

Blue Causeway shows the use of polymer emulsion on unstretched, unprimed raw canvas. If oils had been used the work would have a limited life because of the tendency of the traditional medium to rot raw canvas.

Miss Frankenthaler's application of the emulsion is an excellent example of the medium used for its unique qualities of esthetic expression; a water medium applied in a very fluid manner and resulting in depth as well as transparency.

Color Plate 6. RED SKIRT, by Wallace Bassford, Medium: *Liquitex*. (Collection: Peter Behrens, Hamburg, Germany.)

"Red Skirt," says the artist about this painting, "is the result of three thinly under-painted compositions—one painted over the other. They are all figure schemes, with abstract background forms enveloping the obvious boudoir subject. All three varied somewhat in form, stance, and location within the picture plane and gradually evolved into the interpretation as seen in the completed painting, which includes portions of each.

"In using *Liquitex* Polymer Medium it was desirable to work on a firm, well-tauted canvas surface—one with toothiness, and flatly primed. In this case a good grade of ready-primed Belgian linen canvas was used.

"During the several stages in the picture's paint development, various sizes of brushes were used, as were crushed paper-towel wads to achieve large broad areas, thumb or fingers for certain effects, and painting knives for heavy pigmentation of very flat, smooth passages.

"At all times the *Liquitex* medium was continuously blended with pigments from the jars. [Bassford prepares a jar of one-third water and two-thirds medium for this use. A small amount of color is placed on the palette and mixed. The brush is dipped into the media jar and then into the color. Only clean brushes are placed into the media jar.] Water was added as needed for easy, adaptable consistency. When the painting reached the point of *stop*, a final brushing on of the varnish medium brought the colors to the desired permanent gloss patina."

Color Plate 7. CHILD RUNNING, 39×28 inches, by Russell Woody, 1962. Medium: *Liquitex*.

The reverse side of Masonite was used for this painting—the side with a textured surface. This can sometimes be used to advantage, although the texture is too mechanically regular for most work. To reduce the regularity in this case, the surface was given a coat of modeling paste, which in turn was scraped into a pattern with a large putty knife.

The entire painting was done with very little color; modeling paste, which produces an off-white was used as the major color and for impasto. The paste was mixed with Polymer Medium until it had a creamy, brushable consistency. Application was with various sizes of bristle brushes. When brushed on in this manner, modeling paste has a very pleasing quality; it can be controlled so that textures from coarse to smooth can easily be achieved.

In *Child Running*, even the blue and the white glazes were based on the paste mixture, which was thinned to transparency with medium.

Color Plate 8. LURANAH, 24×33 inches, by Russell Woody, 1962. Medium: *Liquitex*.

This is a portrait of my daughter. The first steps I used in painting it followed traditional methods. A Masonite panel was sanded and given four coats of synthetic gesso. Each layer was brushed counter to the previous one and given a light sanding with fine sandpaper. The gesso was thinned slightly with water.

A detailed drawing of the figure was done on the gesso with fine charcoal. The charcoal was fixed with a spray of polymer medium and water in a ratio of one to one. Spraying was accomplished with a mouth atomizer. Thin washes of color were added. The color design of the whole painting was quickly established by this method.

Then all colors were mixed to a thick consistency with modeling paste and polymer medium and applied with various bristle brushes. Although the painting was very heavy, no palette knives were used. All but the face was established completely in this manner. Glazes on the face and in a few adjacent areas completed the portrait.

portrait: the reestablishing of a pure ground. When areas became too busy or overworked, she painted them over with white to retain freshness and luminosity of color and then reworked the offending passages. Grounds may be reestablished many times before a painting is completed.

Milton Resnick is a painter who has always had unusual sensitivity about the materials he works with. In his early years, this sensitivity took a negative approach; he tried to kill the quality of the medium, and he used house paints because they were less insistent than artists' oils. If the house paints had any semblance of life of their own, he would use additives to destroy the oil quality. Today, however, he is immensely concerned with the plastic qualities of his materials; shallowness or thickness, transparency or opacity, etc., and he creates paintings by responding to the qualities of his media. "Now," he says, "I consider medium to be an animal to ride instead of a dead horse. There is a poetry in crawling paint; a paint not rolled out as if with a steam roller."

In 1959 Resnick began a series of very large paintings in which he wanted to be able to work fast in order to achieve a sense of immediacy. He purchased a fifty-yard roll of paper and cut off a large piece of it for each painting. Some paintings were as long as eighteen feet. Those illustrated in Color Plate 4 (Page 31) and Figure 7, called *Template* and *Capricorn*, are seventy-four by forty-two inches and ninety-six by twenty-three inches, respectively. The paintings were done flat on the floor of his 5000-square-foot studio. To see these vertically he tacked long sticks to the ends so they could be picked up and placed against the wall. When a painting was completed, it was backed on canvas.

Polymer emulsion was chosen as the medium because of its fast application. He used very little paint, but the paintings achieved a sensation of a heavy surface, almost at times having an impasto effect in their projection. These paintings are reminiscent of the sensitive application and empathy the impressionists had for paint quality.

In another experiment with synthetics, Resnick used synthetic cloth supports such as orlon instead of paper or

FIGURE 7

Figure 7. CAPRICORN, 96×23 inches, by Milton Resnick, 1960. Medium: *Liquitex*. (Courtesy: Howard Wise Gallery, New York.)

The search for a paint that would produce an immediate effect, with no waiting periods, and for a responsive size for his paintings led to Milton Resnick's use of *Liquitex* on paper of various dimensions. Resnick wanted no aging to insert itself between the painting act and the final result. The synthetic medium's fast drying and manipulative features made it ideal for this purpose.

As in *Template* (Color Plate 4), the artist's technique was direct, spontaneous, reactive, yet controlled. The paper was stretched on the floor and painted flat; sticks were attached to the ends of the paper so it could be placed upright against a wall to be seen vertically.

In this manner Resnick completed a whole series of paintings.

Figure 8. PORTRAIT, 18×24 inches, by Larry Quackenbush, 1960. Medium: *Liquitex*. (Collection: Mr. and Mrs Julian Yantis—portrait of their daughter.)

With tempered Masonite coated with *Liquitex* Gesso and finely sandpapered as his support, artist Larry Quackenbush usually starts a portrait by making an accurate outline drawing of his model in charcoal and then rendering the important areas in tone with an HB pencil. Says he: "I then go over the rest of the charcoal with pencil and brush off the remaining charcoal with a soft rag or tissue. With a wide, flat, sable watercolor brush, I apply a coat of polymer medium, thinned with water, over the pencil drawing. While the medium will appear 'milky' on first application, it will dry transparent.

"I use *Liquitex* colors and my wide, flat brush to apply paint as transparent washes over the pencil-rendering, in much the same manner as I would apply glazes over an oil underpainting.

"I further develop the painting, as I have this one, by building up the transparent washes, overlapping color on color, at all times making a special effort to further the over-all effect I am trying to achieve. When I reach the stage of the painting where it resembles a rather loosely done watercolor, I begin to build up the important areas of the painting in a semi-opaque manner. Edges are softened and blended with water and medium. I do not hesitate to use my fingers to achieve my desired result. I use no cross-hatching for blending.

"I make a conscious effort to leave the unimportant parts of the painting very loose. To create a feeling of movement through the painting, I apply a light-colored opaque paint over dark areas, using a swirling action of the brush. While the color is still wet, I further the design movement by 'pushing' the color around with the heel or side of my hand. The end result is a sort of ethereal 'smoky' feeling. The spontaneous effect achieved seems to breathe life into the figure.

"In the case of this portrait, to heighten the casual effect of the over-all feeling I have dripped or spattered some *Liquitex* solvent on the painting and quickly blotted it before it penetrated the lower layers of paint.

"There is no reason I can see for varnishing the painting—I like the matte finish of the paint."

Figure 9. AFRICAN VIOLET, 16×20 inches, by Larry Quackenbush, 1960. Medium: *Liquitex*. (Collection: Mr. and Mrs. Donald Stone.)

Although this painting is not a direct portrait, Larry Quackenbush used the same technical means in painting it that he describes in connection with his *Portrait* (Figure 8). *African Violet* was entered in three different shows under three different media categories: It was accepted as a watercolor, a casein and an oil. In each case the judges were evidently sure that the painting had been accomplished in the traditional media and with the traditional techniques.

FIGURE 8

FIGURE 9

canvas. These were tried because of their luminous quality and because of the sheen they gave to the emulsion colors. A monolithic painting was the idea; support and painting completely synthetic and harmonious. His wife, artist Pat Passlof, also made some paintings in this way.

In Resnick's current paintings he returned to oil and canvas. He felt that the bright polymer emulsion colors were beginning to overpower his paintings. His forte today is not brilliant color; in fact he almost reduces or subdues colors. But his synthetic techniques may suit other artists very well.

The romantic realism of Wallace Bassford is in strong contrast to Resnick's abstractions. He has developed his own method of using polymer emulsions. He prepares a large jar of one part water to two parts polymer medium, and places a small amount of color from the paint jar on the palette. In painting, he dips his brush first into the water-and-medium mixture and then into color. Commercially primed Belgian linen canvas is used in this very direct paint-method. A great amount of knife work

goes into Bassford's paintings, especially when thick applications and flat smooth passages are evident as in our example, *Red Skirt* (Color Plate 6, page 34).

Bassford's technique resembles that used in oils to a great extent. He is an outstanding portrait artist, and his portraits in acrylic emulsion are especially eloquent disprovers of the often-heard doubt about the polymer temperas—that they cannot be used in a realistic manner.

That misconception is again disproved by the free but fully detailed portraits by Larry Quackenbush (Figures 8 and 9). Quackenbush started using polymer emulsions to alleviate the problem of having to wait for his under-painting to dry in order that glazing could be accomplished.

Quackenbush used Masonite for his supports, coated with three coats of gesso. He allows the gesso to set overnight and then polishes the surface with very fine waterproof sandpaper, dipping the sandpaper in water and with a rotary motion sanding the gesso to a high gloss finish.

He begins a portrait by making a charcoal drawing in outline from the model. Important areas such as head and hands are then rendered in tone with an HB pencil. The rest of the outline is gone over with the pencil, and the remaining charcoal brushed away with a soft rag or tissue. A fix of polymer medium thinned with water is applied with a flat, wide sable brush.

This classic beginning is then painted over with loose washes and glazes of polymer emulsion color, built from transparent to semi-opaque. Quackenbush does not hesitate to use his fingers or the palm of his hand in pushing the paint around, creating a very spontaneous feeling. Polymer emulsion solvent is sometimes even splashed onto the surface and quickly wiped off to dissolve portions of the paint. A freely expressed realism is the result.

Quackenbush uses an aqua palette. It is a set of porous ceramic paint wells with plastic tops lined with felt. The wells have a wick at both ends and are set into a water reservoir. This eliminates drying of the colors, keeping them quite moist while he works. He mixes his paints on a white enamel tray.

Quackenbush has exhibited many of his polymer paintings as watercolors, oils and caseins. One of his paintings was entered at different times in all three categories—proving the versatility of the medium and its properties, not to mention the difficulties in cataloguing the medium's effects.

Exactness and precise control typify the hard edge, Tenth Street expressionists. In this type of painting, a medium is needed which will give sharply defined cut lines, areas, and stripes of color. There is also a necessity to have a paint that, when applied thinly, produces complete matteness and full, brilliant color. This combination of qualities would be very hard to control in oils, but polymer emulsions are ideal, Nicholas Krushenik, one of the outstanding young artists in the hard edge movement, started using polymer emulsion paints in 1960 for these purposes.

He states that he could not now go back to oils.

Krushenik paints on a gesso ground applied directly to raw canvas. Sometimes a coat of matte medium or Titanium White is painted over (or used instead of) the gesso in order to reduce the pull and semi-absorbent properties of gesso. Emulsion colors with a little water are painted very flatly over the ground. Many of his paintings, such as the one illustrated here (Figure 10), have many coats and shifts of areas before the painting is completed.

Helen Frankenthaler has used the polymer emulsions for their special aqueous quality. She approached the emulsions for a reason different from that of most artists: "Many surprising things—both good and bad—can happen when one forces oneself to change or play around with new paint mediums or techniques," she says. "I wanted to

experiment with a different paint—other than oils."

Miss Frankenthaler usually works on unsized canvas. Because of this she wanted to investigate a paint that was supposed to be more durable than oils on that surface. The unique results and techniques of her investigations can be seen in *Low Tide* (Figure 11) and *Blue Causeway* (Color Plate 5, page 31).

The different styles of paintings discussed in this chapter, all done with acrylic emulsion paints in direct applications, without admixtures, only begin to suggest the varieties of expression that can be achieved when polymer emulsions are used with an effort to turn their own special characteristics to esthetic advantage. The treatments described here may well be considered a point of departure for the reader, encouraging him to develop his own methods and techniques.

Figure 10. PAINTING 1963, 45×45 inches, by Nicholas Krushenik, 1963. Medium: *Liquitex*. (Courtesy: the artist.)

The synthetic aqueous emulsions are especially suited to the paintings of Nicholas Krushenik and to the hard-edge abstractionist school to which he belongs. The emulsions give the precisely controlled, sharp lines and the flat brilliant areas of color typical of this type of painting. Krushenik states that he cannot get the sustained brilliancy and matte quality with any other medium.

This particular painting was done on raw linen canvas primed with *Liquitex* Gesso. Six to eight coats of paint followed in the process of shifting and re-shifting the composition. A little water was added to the colors to achieve smooth brushing qualities. The blue, red, oranges, and blacks of the painting are very flat, very matte, very intense in color. No final varnish was given.

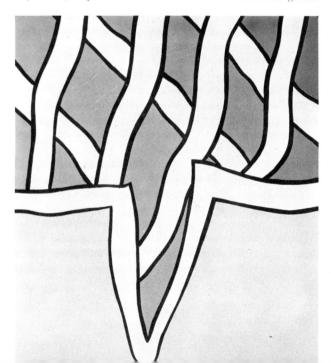

Figure 11. LOW TIDE, 81¾×84 inches, by Helen Frankenthaler, 1963. Medium: *Aqua-Tec*. (Courtesy: the artist and Andre Emmerich Gallery, Inc., New York.)

Similar to *Blue Causeway* (Color Plate 5) in the fluid quality that Helen Frankenthaler has exploited using the aqueous synthetic, *Low Tide* is an example of what an outstanding artist can accomplish when experiencing and developing a new medium; not to emulate or repeat traditional media techniques, but to explore the possibilities of new and characteristic expression.
The painting is on raw canvas.

Chapter 4 / Use of Polymer Emulsions as an Oil Medium

Oil painting is as varied as the artists who use it. Painters can duplicate the many effects and handling techniques of the time-honored oil medium with polymer emulsions in three ways: by using polymer emulsion tube colors, or by adding gel or modeling paste to the jar colors. The success of the polymer emulsions in emulating oils can be seen in the fact that synthetic paintings are often exhibited as "oil paintings."

Tube Colors. The most facile method of duplicating the brushing and handling characteristics of oil paint is to use thick, polymer emulsion tube colors. The tube colors in most trade lines—both acrylic and copolymer—have the same body as an oil paint and the paint blends, mixes on the palette, holds sharp brush and knife configurations, and, in general, manipulates exactly like oils. The difference between oil paints and polymer emulsion tube colors is the faster drying time and the advantages already outlined of plastic paint over oil.

The recent introduction of the polymer emulsion tube colors to the art market does away with the objections many artists have had when working with the polymer emulsions: that they did not allow enough time for color blendings on the canvas, and that paint dried too quickly on the palette. Most brands of tubed emulsions can be worked for a day on the canvas, but dry overnight. In thin applications the paints dry within thirty minutes to an hour.

Tube colors can be mixed with water to create wash techniques as well as impastos and any manipulation between the two. Therefore, an impression of mixed media techniques can be achieved in one work using only one medium. Of course, when the tube paints are thinned with water or mediums they dry faster.

Gel. Another method of obtaining oil paint characteristics with polymer emulsion is to add a gel medium to the jar colors. The amount of gel used depends on the intent of the artist, and every artist should experiment with various mixtures to find out what proportion of gel to color suits his various purposes. A mixture of one part gel to two parts color is perhaps the most commonly used. This proportion produces a soft buttery consistency that has pull and viscosity without perceptibly affecting the opacity or the strength of the color. (See gel manipulation in Figure 1.) Crisp brush strokes, painting knife configurations, impastos are easily done.

The gel addition slows down the drying time of the emulsions, and this increases the working time. Plastic colors as they come from the jar dry in five to ten minutes; with gel they take from fifteen to more than thirty minutes to reach surface hardness, depending on how much gel is added. Thus, colors can be blended on the canvas, as with oil paints, and wet painting can extend into hours. Painting time is not as great as with tube colors, however.

When gel is used in a ratio greater than one part gel to two parts color, the gel, which is milky in color, whitens the color somewhat when wet, and the true color will not become apparent until it has dried. This calls for a certain psychological adjustment on the part of the artist, who must learn from experience exactly how colors in various mixtures change when they dry. The best method of assuring the proper color and texture is to test a gel-color mixture on a separate surface before applying it to a painting.

Color density is not appreciably reduced when gel is used in the one-to-two ratio. Greater amounts of gel, however, render the colors increasingly transparent. This trait, incidentally, permits an unusual three-dimensional glaze technique. When a small amount of color is mixed with gel and the resulting paint applied in a heavy manner with brush or knife, a thick but transparent layer of color is achieved. (See Figure 1—F.) This is only one of many new painting effects possible with gel-

Figure 12. YOUNG MAN IN A BULLFIGHTER'S CAPE, 24 × 18 inches, by Russell Woody, 1963. Medium: *Liquitex*.

In this sketch, extruded line from a squeeze bottle has been left unadorned. The work was painted on heavy watercolor paper, with the white of the paper as a background: only the dark areas are paint.

The lines of the head and cape were quickly drawn in black, and the upper left corner in a combination of extruded black and red line. After thirty minutes, the lines were dry, and the blue-black cape was painted, as were the brilliant red scarf and the red area immediately behind the head. The sketch was pressed to a Masonite panel, with *Liquitex* Polymer Medium providing the adhesive.

The work was given a protective coat of gloss medium as a final varnish, which has allowed me to wash the paper innumerable times without the work being hurt in the least. This has proved of great help, for I have used *Young Man in a Bullfighter's Cape* in many demonstrations of technique, and it has passed through hundreds of hands.

Figure 13. AN AMBULANCE WENT BY, 24×48 inches, by Russell Woody, 1963. Medium: *Liquitex*.

Masonite was turned to the rough side for this extruded-line painting. Washes, glazes, and opaque paint were employed over a preliminary build-up of three-dimensional line. The line, squeezed from a bottle, consisted of a mixture of one part gel medium, one part modeling paste, and three parts color. Paints were also mixed with modeling paste and gel medium for heavy brush strokes (no knives were used); the impasto paint was worked and re-worked over the understructure, with the painting sometimes being placed in a vertical position, sometimes in its final horizontal format. The final effect is that of very heavily textured oils.

A varnish composed of five parts polymer medium and one part matte varnish was applied to the finished work.

mixed polymer emulsion paints.

Gel medium dries to a high gloss. If this gloss is considered excessive, matte medium may be mixed into the gel. But, in order not to alter the gel's viscous quality, it is better to achieve the matte tone by varnishing over the completed painting with matte varnish or medium than to mix the matte medium into the gel. Matte varnish also reduces pressure sensitivity, which sometimes occurs when a great amount of gel is used.

The gel medium, being a pure polymer emulsion itself, retains the flexibility of the polymer emulsion colors, and thus can be used on canvas, paper, or any other flexible support. Even paintings which contain impastos an inch thick can be rolled without endangering the paints. Rigid supports can of course also be used.

An unusual technique possible with gel permits a working time of up to two hours and produces soft blendings of color of outstanding brilliance. The support is given a coating of pure gel in one-eighth or one-quarter inch thickness. This may be applied with a brush, or with a palette knife if a very smooth surface is desired. A white ground of gesso or Titanium White under the gel coating will add brilliance to the colors. Colors without additions of any kind are then worked into the wet gel with bristle brushes. Colors can be directly blended into the gel "veneer" instead of on the palette. Incomplete blendings of colors create very sparkling effects. If more time is needed, quick sprays of water from an atomizer (old perfume spray bottles work well) will keep the paint workable for hours. Multiple layers of transparent or translucent paint can be built up to create great depths of color that give an actual three-dimensional visual experience. (See Figure 1−G.)

Modeling Paste. Although polymer emulsion tube colors produce the simplest means of emulating oils with synthetics, modeling paste may also be used for a similar purpose. Like gel, modeling paste gives a viscous pull when mixed with colors, but it tints colors slightly. Full pigment intensity begins to be lost when paste is used in greater degrees than one part paste to

Color Plate 9. ADOLESCENT GIRL, 48×24 inches, by Russell Woody, 1962. Medium: *Liquitex.*

Modeling paste was also used in this painting which I began in my usual manner by direct underpainting on a Masonite panel without a size or ground (the underpainting itself serves as a ground). Paints were thinned with polymer medium. No water was used, in order that a better bind between paint and support could be achieved. Underpainting was done in red tints to complement the greens and blues which were to follow, though very little red shows through in the finished work.

Colors were mixed with modeling paste and directly applied with a large putty knife. A small amount of brush work completed the painting.

It was given a final gloss varnish of polymer medium. (Bubbles often occur when the varnish is brushed over heavy impasto. When this happens, as it did in this case, a soft, wide brush will pick the bubbles up if it is wiped over the area *immediately.* If the bubbles are permitted to dry even a bit, a brush will cloud the surface, however. For this reason, it is advisable to varnish a large work by sections, so control can be maintained.)

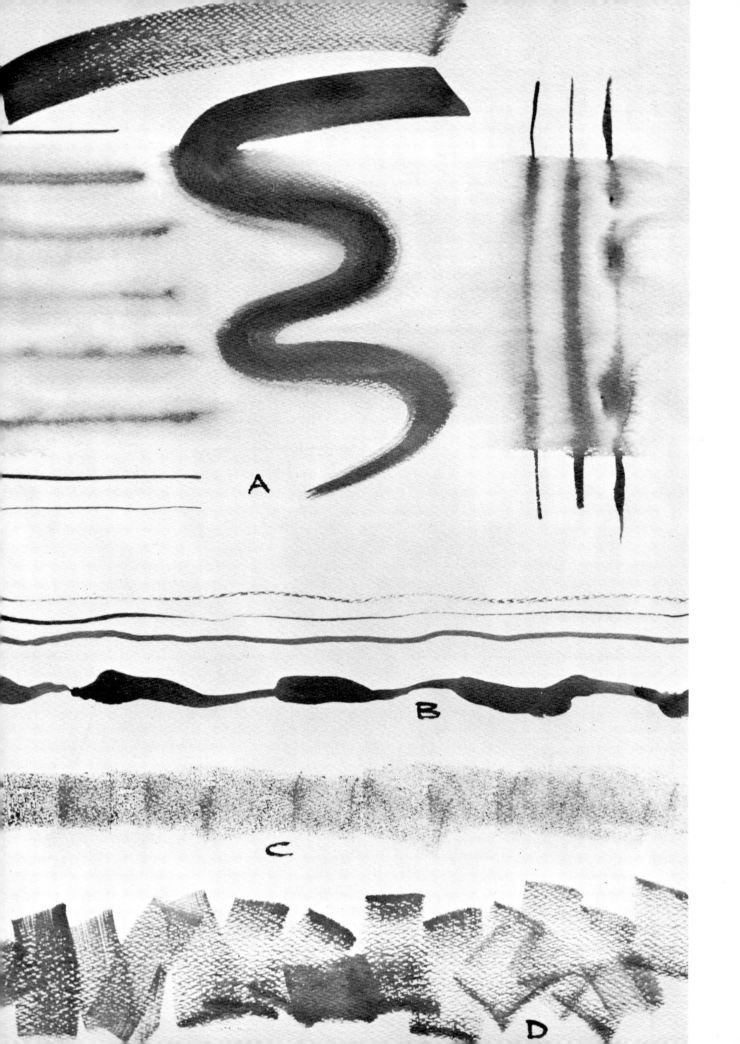

A

B

C

D

E. Here a round stencil brush was held vertically and gently pounced on the paper. The right-hand section shows the result of using the same technique on wet paper.

F. The white tones were drawn in with a white crayon before a wash was applied. The crayon wax created a resist for the water medium. (Many kinds of wax or grease crayons and pencils can be employed for this purpose; so can oils and turpentine painted on with a brush.) The dark lines were drawn over the wash resist.

G. The white "X" shows how completely and easily a ground can be reestablished and corrected with synthetic paints. A few strokes of Titanium White almost immediately covered a section of the dry watercolor. As soon as it dried again, painting could continue. In watercolors, this process allows for corrections and manipulations impossible with the traditional medium.

H. This figure was sketched in with conté crayon, and broad washes of color were applied over it. The polymer emulsions are excellent for wash drawings over almost any graphic media.

I. An over-all wash was given to this section of paper. While the wash was wet, the end of the watercolor brush (pointed with a knife) was used to draw into the medium. The depression in the wet paper caused fluid color to collect and create a soft line. The broad white lines were scratched in with a razor blade after the wash dried.

J. A dry-brush demonstration showing the repetitive strokes by which an artist can produce almost any degree of shade or opacity.

for weeks, but it also permits two unique techniques. Washes of transparent color can be made over painted grounds without picking up the underlying work, giving a sense of depth and multiple layers to a painting. Or a thin opaque wash or two of Titanium White may be applied, which will completely cover the work underneath and present a new white surface on which to work.

This latter technique can also be employed to tone down certain areas or provide atmospheric mannerisms. If it is used consistently throughout a painting, the result is a gouache: a water medium in which no transparent colors are used. If a gouache effect is intended, the more opaque colors are recommended. Traditionally, gouache could not be piled up heavily or it would crack. The plastic paints permit any amount of dense paint films without cracking; they remain completely flexible even on very light weight paper.

Watercolor hues are lighter when they dry than they appear when wet. This holds true also with the polymer temperas when mixed with a generous quantity of water and used transparently. Used with less water for a more opaque effect, they hold their color hue. Polymer colors in general are more brilliant when dry than the natural media.

Some polymer emulsion colors show pigment separation when they are diluted too freely with water. This is frequently caused by the artist having diluted the colors too much in the jars, either by dipping into them with a wet brush or by adding water on top to keep colors from forming skins. The reason for pigment separation is a loss of medium. If this occurs on the palette or on the paper, a few drops of matte medium will correct the fault. The earth pigments are the most vulnerable in this regard, and the degree of vulnerability varies since the earth colors derive from various levels and places in the earth.

The artist need not limit himself to the usual watercolor brushes when using polymer emulsions. Oil bristle brushes, stippling brushes, palette knives, sticks, sponges, rags, and other implements can be used to advantage. I probably use more oil brushes than

Figure 15. PENNY, 30×22 inches, by Russell Woody, 1962. Medium: *Liquitex*.

In this study, the synthetic emulsion was handled as a traditional-type watercolor wash. The lines were first drawn in with water-thinned Mars Black; a homemade reed pen was the drawing implement. Washes of color over the dry, roughly textured watercolor paper completed the work. (I mixed a tube of Cadmium Yellow watercolor paint with the *Liquitex* colors, because I happened to be out of the emulsion Cadmium at the time. The aqueous synthetics may be combined with most other water-based colors, including temperas and caseins, and they impart the synthetics' characteristics of permanency and adhesion to the media to which they are added.) A coat of *Liquitex* Matte Varnish was then applied to protect the unpainted paper as well as retain the matte quality of a watercolor.

I have used this work as a technical example in lectures I have given on the synthetics. Because of constant handling, it has had to be washed several times with soap and water, yet no damage is evident.

Figure 16. Study for BALLET, 30×22 inches, by Russell Woody, 1963. Medium: *Liquitex*.

Liquitex Mars Black was diluted with water and used as an ink for this quick sketch. The paint was mixed in a small glass jar so that a bamboo pen could be dipped into the synthetic ink. The same black was diluted with more water on the palette and applied as a wash with a broad, flat watercolor brush. A small amount of medium was added to the thin black so that the pigment particles would not separate if too much water was inadvertently added.

When a pen is used with the synthetic emulsions, the same precaution must be observed as with brushes; the implement must be kept wet, or the plastic will dry and render it useless. One reason I like to use a bamboo pen in drawing with the emulsions is that the plastic can easily be scraped off the wood with a knife, and the pen can be resharpened.

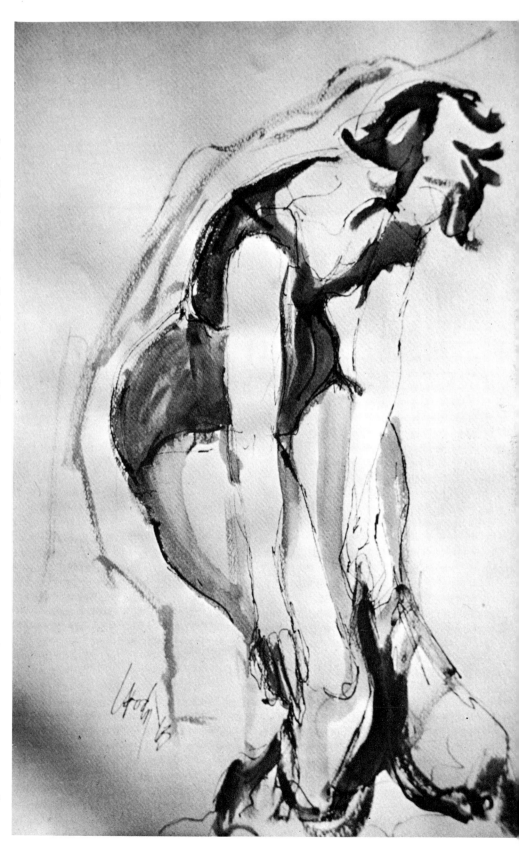

Figure 17. TIDEWATER, 15×6 inches, by Barclay Sheaks, 1963. Medium: *Liquitex.* (Courtesy: the artist.)

Traditional watercolor effects are apparent in this painting, yet they were achieved with an acrylic emulsion. Such a synthetic has some definite advantages over the older watercolor medium. The color is more vibrant, for one thing; translucent as well as opaque colors are easily established, even on a wet stock or in a wet area; and the painting is not dissolved by water after it dries, which gives much more protection to the finished work.

Here Barclay Sheaks has worked with a wet-in-wet process. Heavy watercolor paper was first saturated with a half-and-half mixture of water and *Liquitex* medium. When this had throughly soaked into the surface, he began his painting with washes of *Liquitex* color thinned with water. The paints feathered and spread in the normal watercolor manner. Semi-opaque color was applied over this and controlled by blotting and tilting the board to establish the desired flow. The final opaque accents were painted in while the paper was still moist.

After the work was dry, it was given a coat of semi-matte varnish, made by mixing matte varnish with gloss polymer medium to the desired degree of gloss, to protect the painting and to give an over-all sheen.

soft sables in painting a polymer watercolor. The minute an artist decides a painting must be executed in a certain mechanical method with the correctly prescribed set of tools, he restricts his imagination unnecessarily. Techniques are only a means to an end, and they should not hamper creative expression.

All the usual watercolor "tricks" can be used with the emulsions. Materials to repel water may be applied to paper to achieve a white space, a clearly defined line, or splotching. (See Figures 14 – F and 29). Rubber cement, turpentine, wax, crayons, clear oils, and oil pastels or pencils are a few of the media used in resist techniques. Masking out with tapes and stencils, and scratching in white lines and areas with knives or razor blades may be desired in certain situations. The variety is limited only by the ingenuity of the artist.

Preliminary sketches in pencil, ink, charcoal, or plastic color can enhance a watercolor at times. Graphic media should be fixed with a spray of matte medium or varnish to keep them from bleeding or smearing. Mix the medium about half and half with water and spray through a mist atomizer or air gun in a back and forth motion.

A drawing in thinned emulsion colors may sometimes be desired, and it needs no fixing after it is dry. (See Figures 15 and 16). The drawing will not run or feather, even if the paper is thoroughly saturated for a wet watercolor painting over the sketch. Thin

colors can be applied with a bamboo or quill pen as well as with fine line brushes or a palette knife for preliminary drawing. A sharpened stick dipped into the emulsion colors will effect excellent and unusual lines.

Another type of linear definition can be accomplished in the wet-in-wet technique. Color applied to water-saturated paper immediately diffuses, and it is impossible to paint in a hard line. Drawing can be done at this stage by using an instrument such as the sharpened point of a watercolor brush or a stick, depending on whether a fine or broad line is desired. Drawing in this manner on the soft, wet paper creates shallow depressions in which previously applied wet color deposits. Within fifteen seconds a very pleasing indented line results. (See Figure 14 – I.)

Artist and teacher Barclay Sheaks had never been enthusiastic about watercolor painting until he started using polymer emulsion paints. He was interested in a more translucent or opaque quality than watercolor usually achieved, and he developed his polymer technique with the objective of combining a certain opacity with the soft, immediate and spontaneous effect so characteristic of watercolor. (See Figure 17.)

Sheaks first saturates the paper with polymer medium or matte medium (depending on whether he wants a more brilliant surface and sheen or a more matte effect) cut to half strength with water. Time must be given to permit the medium to soak into the surface. Two or three coats of medium and water might be necessary to achieve a coat that will stay relatively workable over a period of several hours. If drying is too rapid a fine spray of water from an atomizer will keep the paper at the right saturation point.

Emulsion colors mixed to a watercolor consistency may then be employed to quickly establish basic color shapes and values. Semi-opaque color is applied over this and controlled by blotting and tilting the board to accomplish the desired flow. Areas can be picked up with a dry brush for highlighting and correcting. Final accents of straight plastic color are added, if desired. Sheaks protects his paintings with a final coat of matte varnish, gloss medium or both. To avoid brush marks, the final varnish should be diluted with water and a soft brush used in its application.

Air bubbles often form in mixtures of polymer medium and water as a result of too-vigorous brush work. A dry brush will easily pick up the bubbles with one deft stroke. Some artists have actually used these bubbles to create textural emphasis. (See Figure 6 and Color Plate 23, page 99.)

The polymer emulsions are especially well suited for sketching or field trips. They can be packed in a small tackle box for easy carrying. Many artists often make a watercolor painting "on location" and later render the work in oils in the studio. With polymer emulsions, the artist can create his "oil" painting directly on his watercolor; there is no need for laborious transferal of the work to another surface, since the same basic medium is used in both the watercolor and oil techniques. Actually, the artist can even use impasto oil techniques on field trips, because he can roll the work after the short time it takes to dry.

Chapter 6 / Use as Tempera and Casein

Tempera. Most polymer emulsion paints as they come from the jar have an appearance somewhere between that of the egg-base tempera medium and the milk-base casein medium. The synthetic paint can be used to achieve the effects of both of these traditional media.

In pure egg tempera painting, pigment ground in water is mixed with the yolk of an egg just prior to application. The egg yolk, which serves as a binder vehicle, gives an opalescent or iridescent semi-gloss finish which is the essence of the tempera medium. The colors can run the gamut from transparent to opaque, but the most characteristic tempera quality is a glowing translucence.

Egg tempera has certain drawbacks in durability, however. Rigid panel supports should be used in order to prevent cracking, which very often results when tempera is applied in thick or multiple layers on any support. Water redissolves the medium, atmospheric conditions can cause harm, and mold lives on the egg binder.

The best characteristics of egg tempera minus all of its drawbacks can be obtained with the use of the synthetic emulsions. The advantages of the synthetics are numerous: colors and paint films do not pick up when over-painted, corrections can be made by painting out an area in white, an indefinite number of paint layers can be built up without danger of cracking, the finished painting is not subject to damage by water or scratching or dirt, blending of colors is more easily achieved, impastos can be applied, and flexible supports may be used because the paint remains pliable after drying.

There are two basic techniques of tempera painting with the synthetics, one actually using an egg, the other duplicating tempera effects with the emulsions alone. In the egg technique, the yolk is separated from the white by pouring the raw egg back and forth between two glasses, allowing the white to drain and keeping the yolk sac intact. All of the white need not be so carefully removed as in pure egg tempera. The skin of the yolk is then broken and its contents poured into a container with a lid. The egg can be used for about three days without spoiling.

Polymer emulsion colors are mixed with the yolk in the proportions of one or two parts yolk to three parts color. In painting, brushes are dipped into water and then into the egg-and-color mixture. More water should be used for greater transparency or to keep the paint from pulling or drying too fast. Warm water seems to facilitate the blending. The yellow of the yolk may darken some colors and give a yellowish cast to white, but sunlight bleaches this out in a short time.

Luminosity, so typical of egg tempera, is enhanced by using a white or very light ground. A panel of fine woven canvas or sanded Masonite should be coated with four to six coats of plastic gesso. The gesso should be thinned with water and each coat lightly sanded with fine waterproof sandpaper that has been moistened with water. Colors are then painted in very transparent washes and gradually proceed to layers of translucent and opaque paint. All the traditional tempera techniques may be used, such as underpainting in a tone complementary to the overpainting—a green undertone, for example, strengthens and intensely activates a final red. A coat of matte varnish may be applied to a finished painting to protect the thin films of color if desired.

The Old Masters usually began their tempera paintings with a very detailed drawing, and this technique can still be used to advantage. Pencil, hard charcoal, or light inks may be used. It is a good idea to fix these with a light spray of matte medium diluted with two-thirds water.

Thomas Hart Benton uses the egg-

Figure 18. GREEN BOTTLE, 24×30 inches, by William E. Preston, 1963. Medium: *Liquitex*. (Collection: Mr. and Mrs. Leon Perkins.)

In talking about his painting *On the Ledge* (Color Plate 12), William Preston has described his basic technique. In this work, all the light areas were painted with opaque colors, while all the shadows are translucent glazes. The title *Green Bottle* comes from the brilliant color (unfortunately not apparent in this black-and-white reproduction) of the bottle in the window, which is lighted from behind. The other colors in the painting are muted earths and bands of red, the latter encircling some of the hanging buoys.

Figure 19. TIDE POOL, 16×20 inches, by William E. Preston, 1963. Medium: *Liquitex*. (Collection: Judge and Mrs. Lawrence Duncan.)

Tide Pool, although at first glance a realistic rendering of a section of a shallow pool, nonetheless has an abstract design to it. This black-and-white reproduction almost makes the work appear a complete abstraction. The transparent glazes are so thin that they can hardly be seen without their color values. The colors are predominantly earths with grey-blue and muted green overlays that give the painting depth. Preston's technical process is basically that which he used for *On the Ledge*. (Color Plate 12).

Color Plate 12. ON THE LEDGE, 20×26 inches, by William E. Preston, 1963. Medium: *Liquitex*. (Collection: Mr. Paul Guillmette.)

The magic realist paintings of William Preston show how synthetic emulsion paints can be used to give transparent-translucent tempera effects.

"All my work," says Preston, "is done on Masonite panels. I find using *Liquitex* the most logical extension of the watercolor technique because, besides its watercolor qualities, it provides many of those of oil, including the opportunity for pigment development. The contrast of transparent with opaque areas it permits is of great interest to me, and I find the color obtained by the building up of many layers of transparent paint fascinating. I have long worked in water color and used to use egg tempera. Now I continue my work in watercolor and *Liquitex*.

"My technique is mostly based on working habits formed by my experience with egg tempera and is as follows:

"I give the panel about six or eight coats of *Liquitex* gesso, sanded down in between. I then do my drawing on the panel with pencil or charcoal. I start painting with thin transparent color washes (thinned with water only), gradually making them darker and darker in value—but always keeping the whole painting transparent, just as in a watercolor. Sometimes these first washes are in colors complementary to the final colors, sometimes not. I use very few colors directly from the jar, mixing the subtle tones I prefer on the palette before application. I don't hesitate to splatter, throw paint, use sponges, knives, etc. (During this stage, the ability to reestablish areas with white keeps the painting quite flexible.) I then isolate the underpainting with a coat of Matte Medium. After this is dry, I start to scumble all areas down to a mid-point of transparency known as opalescence—not fully transparent, not fully opaque.

"I continue to work, controlling the degree of transparency, pulling my shadows down to full transparency, making my lights fully opaque.

"My palette is a sheet of glass, and I use the following colors: Raw Siena, Burnt Umber, Ultramarine Blue, Cerulean Blue, Phthalocyanine Blue, Hookers Green, Phthalocyanine Green, Black, Indo Orange, Cadmium Red Light, Cadmium Orange, Yellow Oxide, Cadmium Yellow Pale, Napthol Crimson, Cadmium Yellow Medium."

base synthetic tempera technique for his easel paintings. The transparency and the resulting sense of depth that the medium achieves suit his work very well.

Synthetic media alone can create a painting in the egg tempera process and to similar effects. The support should be prepared with gesso as described earlier, and the detailed drawing done on this ground. Washes of color thinned to a watercolor consistency are applied over the drawing in continuing layers until the values of the painting are established. At this point the high lights and strong opaques are added. Further glazing is done with colors which have been diluted with matte medium. Such effects as stippling, splattering, or fine detail should be completed before the final glazes are applied.

Transparency is the touchstone of this type of painting. Colors, washes, and glazes must be kept clear and precise, imparting the luminous, fluid immediacy that egg tempera gives. If a passage becomes too cloudy or glazes become too thick, the original ground can be reestablished with one or two light coats of white. Fine lines and delicate detail are easily achieved with small watercolor sables. The paint holds an edge and will not bleed.

William Preston's magic realist paintings which reflect the atmosphere of the York Village, Maine, countryside where he lives, are done in this synthetic tempera technique. (See Figures 18, 19, and Color Plate 12, opposite.) The young artist does not hesitate to move the paint around, scumbling, stippling, using knife work, and even throwing paint at times. The images created carry with them an abstract as well as a naturalistic quality. He states that he was somewhat shy of the polymer emulsion when he first started using it and it took him some time to assimilate the new approach and different technical manipulations possible, but today he finds the synthetics the most satisfactory medium.

John C. Pellew, an instructor at the Famous Artists School in Westport, Connecticut, and primarily a watercolorist, begins many paintings in a watercolor manner on gesso panels and then finishes them in a tempera

technique using fine opaque strokes which completely cover the original watercolor. Pellew uses polymer emulsion with round, sable watercolor brushes from the beginning to the end of such paintings. A month or so of detailed brushing brings each painting to termination, as in *Toward Tintagel* (Figure 20).

Casein. The polymer emulsion paints can achieve casein effects by the addition of other ingredients to the colors (See Figures 21, 22, 23 and 9.) The matte and cream-like quality of casein is produced by adding matte medium to emulsion tube colors.

Some inert clays or modeling paste may be used to achieve a casein body with jar colors. The best of the inert clays are celite and diatomaceous earth; these are types of silica. Whiting (Paris White), which is native calcium carbonate, may also serve. Additives of this sort should not be used in over one-quarter volume or they will tint the pigments or form coarse paints. Enough medium (gloss or matte) should always be added to achieve a flexible paint film if the painting is to be on paper or other flexible supports. In this manner they will also duplicate finger paints and adhere very well to finger paint papers.

Application of polymer emulsions in the casein manner is the same as with traditional casein. Paintings dry in about the same time due to the evaporation of water. Once the paint is dry, it cannot be redissolved or reworked except by overpainting.

Traditional casein cannot be used in impasto or heavy coatings because the paint will crack and peel off the support in time. A synthetic casein, however, can be built up to any thickness without danger. The yellowing of traditional casein does not occur either.

I have used tube caseins mixed with matte medium for contrast in surface sheen. (The emulsions and casein colors are usually compatible.) This process is somewhat easier than augmenting the synthetic with fillers. I have also repaired old casein paintings which have begun to crack with this method. (See Figure 24.) A final coating with matte varnish, incidentally, will completely preserve traditional

Figure 20. TOWARD TINTAGEL, 14×27 inches, by John C. Pellew, 1962. Medium: *Liquitex*. (Collection: Albert Dorne. Photo by Zoltan Henezel, Famous Artists School.)

"Toward Tintagel was painted in my studio from a dry-brush ink sketch and a small watercolor made on the north coast of Cornwall, England, where I was born," says Pellew.

"Four thin coats of *Liquitex* Gesso were given to both sides of a one-eighth-inch Masonite panel to counteract warping.

"The composition was sketched in pencil on tracing paper. At this stage, the figure was only roughed in for size and position. The back of the paper was then rubbed with soft pencil and the drawing traced onto the panel. A careful drawing of the figure (of the actual size it appears in the painting) was then made with a 2H pencil and traced in position on the panel. The pale drawing, or tracing, on the white gesso ground was then gone over with diluted Mars Black *Liquitex*. (I used a No. 0 watercolor brush; round sable watercolor brushes were used throughout—the larger sizes for the first lay-in, which consisted of thin washes of color.)

"The picture at this stage looked like my usual transparent watercolors. From here on it was built up gradually with opaque strokes of color in a tempera technique that completely covered the watercolor-type lay-in. (All of this latter painting was done with various small brushes, No. 1 being most used.)

"My palette consisted of White, Yellow Ocher, Raw Siena, Burnt Umber, Cadmium Red, light Cerulean Blue, and Mars Black. All my greens were mixtures. The painting took about a month to do."

Figure 21. SELF PORTRAIT, 28×22 inches, by Russell Woody, 1962. Medium: *Liquitex*.

Mat board was employed as a support for this self portrait. *Liquitex* paints in their original consistency were applied over the board in a semi-casein technique. The paper absorbed a good deal of the water in the paints and made dry brushing almost necessary. In this case, I wanted the drying pull of the paint. If I had not, I would have used a coat of gesso or matte medium to eliminate the fast absorption.

The small amount of line seen is due to the paint having been pushed around the surface with a palette knife.

Figure 22. THE KITTIWAKE AND JOHN WALTON 36×36 inches, by Fairfield Porter, 1963. Medium: *Liquitex*. (Courtesy: Tibor di Nagy Gallery, New York. Photo by Ellen Auerbach.)

Fairfield Porter likes the effects of aqueous media such as casein, tempera, and watercolor, and this affinity is reflected in his paintings with *Liquitex*. Here it has enabled him to work on canvas in a casein manner without the traditional medium's disadvantage of cracking. What's more, the synthetic pigments have created new color interplay and contrasts, especially in the pastel shades and tints.

Figure 23. STEPHEN AND KATHY, 60×48 inches, by Fairfield Porter, 1963. Medium: *Liquitex*. (Courtesy: Tibor de Nagy Gallery, New York. Photo by Ellen Auerbach.)

Technically, these figures are handled in a manner similar to that employed in Figure 22. This is another loose, realistic interpretation that helps disprove the idea that the new plastic media cannot be used in the traditional realistic forms.

casein (watercolor, too), as well as give a unified luster to paintings of synthetic casein.

Fairfield Porter is an artist who has been working with polymer emulsion for almost two years. To achieve casein-like effects, he first primes his canvas with plastic gesso or glue, and then paints in a very direct fashion, as in *The Kittiwake and John Walton* and *Stephen and Kathy* (Figures 22 and 23). He employs thin, transparent washes that contrast with opaque, slightly heavier areas. Sometimes Porter mixes matte medium in with the color, along with water, to thin it without creating a textural surface. He does not use a final varnish of gloss medium but allows the paint to remain matte and soft.

Much as he likes the polymer emulsions, Porter says that he has not yet solved all his own technical problems with the medium. He still finds it somewhat distracting, for example, that the colors when greatly thinned with water seem to him to dry lighter than they appear when wet. Just the same, Porter feels that the medium's advantages, such as its permanency, definitely outweigh any drawbacks it may have.

Figure 24. CHAIRS, 38×23 inches, by Russell Woody, 1957. Media: Casein with *Liquitex* varnish.

Heavy areas of casein were applied in this study of chairs—and as a result the medium began to crack and peel about three years after the work had been completed (some of this can still be seen in the upper areas just above the chairs). A varnish of *Liquitex* Medium arrested the condition, however, and the study has not deteriorated in the least since it was varnished with the plastic.

Synthetic emulsion varnishes can be used to protect almost any work or surface that is not oily or does not have a hard shine.

Chapter 7 / Mixed Media Techniques

While polymer emulsions should never be literally mixed with oil paints, the two media can be combined in paintings. Oils may be applied over synthetics as soon as the synthetics are dry. In fact, the synthetics protect the canvas from attack by the oil medium, much as a ground does. The synthetics can be painted over oils, too, but only after the oils have thoroughly dried.

The work of Robert Goodnough is an outstanding example of plastic and oil combinations attuned to the particular objectives of an individual painter. Goodnough's primary preoccupation in painting is to develop evolving forms on the canvas. He first draws a shape — say a boat — with charcoal on primed canvas. Then, working in polymer emulsions, he reworks the shape over and over again. It may remain a boat, or it may become something else, transformed out of the associated ideas and reactions of the artist at work. The shape, and not the object it represents, is paramount, and the whole painting is constantly in flux, changing several times before completion. To record this evolution of an idea, Goodnough

sometimes has photographs taken at several stages. The photograph of *Excursion* (Color Plate 15, page 68) was taken just before the painting was finished. (See also Figures 25 and 26 for related techniques by Goodnough.)

The fast drying qualities of the emulsions help Goodnough in this kind of development of a painting. When the shapes have reached a near-final form, oils are introduced for final emphasis. The contrasting of the matte of the aqueous paints with the gloss of the oils lends great richness and variety to the surface. Sometimes Goodnough masks out certain shapes with masking tape and then fills them in with plastics. Sharply outlined shapes are easily accomplished with the synthetics.

Syd Solomon is another artist who underpaints with polymer emulsions (primarily for the time-saving factor) and applies glazes of oils over them. He sometimes reverses the process and applies emulsions over oils.

This is an unusual technique, but Solomon — who has been working with synthetics since 1940 — has it well under control. *Signal* (Color Plate 13, page 65), and *Rivuleto* (Figure 27),

are examples of two different methods he used in this process. In *Rivuleto*, thin oil glazes were used over polymer colors and lightly rubbed off. Then water-thinned polymer emulsion glazes were brushed over the oil areas to cause a *craze* (fine surface lines in alligator pattern or wrinkles) created because the water medium did not adhere to the oil in places.

Signal has a kind of reconstituted oil under the emulsion overpainting. Oil paints thinned with mineral spirits were first brushed over an absorbent paper. When most of the linseed oil was absorbed, the paint was reactivated with mineral spirits and wiped over the underpainting in a glazing method. This allows the polymer emulsions to adhere readily over an oil-like surface, and gives a rather "oil" look to the synthetics. (I do not recommend this technique as a standard practice, however, since it can reduce the durability of a painting and weaken its adhesive qualities if not carefully done.)

Figure 28 and Color Plate 14 (page 68) illustrate ink used with polymer emulsion in a mixed media application. Figure 29 shows a resist technique.

Figure 25. ULYSSES-AA-P, 84×84 inches, by Robert Good-nough, 1961-62. Media: *Liquitex* and oil. (Courtesy: the artist.)

Ulysses-AA-P is in contrast to Goodnough's *Excursion* (Color Plate 13). Here the painting consists of pure brush strokes. There are no definitive shapes of color which have been outlined, shifted, and juxtaposed. The work is spontaneous in effect, yet recalls cubistic discipline.

As in the color reproduction, the brilliancy and matte quality of the polymer emulsion straight from the jar have been played against the gloss of oil. The work was turned to several sides in the painting process, as the dripping, running, and feathering of the paint indicate. Goodnough does not consciously develop paint effects. If such things as runs occur, he does not work to erase them, but, on the other hand, he does not try to create them, either. He prefers the spontaneity of the paint itself and allows it to work for him.

The painting is on primed commercial canvas.

Figure 26. ABDUCTION (HUMOROUS ABDUCTION NO. 3), 78×78 inches, by Robert Goodnough, 1962. Media: *Liquitex* and oil. (Collection: Richard Brown Baker. Photo by Eric Pollitzer.)

Abduction is similar in technique to *Excursion* (Color Plate 13) except that *Liquitex* has been painted over oil paints in certain areas. Although it is usually not advisable to use the emulsions over oil, it can be done when the oil content has been reduced to effect a non-gloss sheen. In several sections of this work, oil paint has been thinned with turpentine to the point of a matte wash (top center, left, and lower right). *Liquitex* was applied over some of this, and no problems involving durability or adhesion arose.

Figure 27. RIVULETO, 52×36 inches, by Syd Solomon, 1962. Media: *Liquitex* and oil. (Courtesy: Saidenberg Gallery, New York. Photo by John F. Waggaman.)

Rivuleto is unusual in that it incorporates a technique of double glazing.

Linen canvas was given a ground of gesso, as described in the caption for *Signal* (Color Plate 13). Underpainting proceeded directly with *Liquitex* colors. Thin oil paint glazes were applied over this. When the oil glaze was partially dry, it was wiped or lightly rubbed with a cloth to remove excess oil. Then a second (or double) glaze was applied. These final glazes were composed of the water-thinned emulsion. The water-based glazes over the dry oil glazes produced a *craze*—a fine alligator-type separation which effects a thin textural surface. This can be seen especially in the right and bottom portions of *Rivuleto*.

Color Plate 13. SIGNAL, 77×60 inches, by Syd Solomon, 1962. Media: *Liquitex* and oil (with PVA emulsion size). (Courtesy: Rose Art Museum, Brandeis University.)

This is another example of a painting in which the synthetic and oil media are combined.

Raw Belgian linen was used as a support for *Signal*. It was stretched and given a one-coat size of polyvinyl acetate emulsion (*Polymer Tempera*), thinned half-and-half with water. A ground of *Liquitex* Gesso was applied. The first coat of gesso was brushed in a large circle in the center of the canvas to give support to that portion of the painting surface on which Solomon works the most. When the circle was dry, an over-all application of slightly thinned gesso completed the ground.

The painting was begun with very thin washes and stains of several inks and dyes. With color patterns established, the various planes were emphasized with *Liquitex* colors. Textures were then built with the opaque paints. Glazes followed, and the painting was taken to a point near completion with these. Final glazing was accomplished with oil paints. So that a final emulsion varnish would remain effective over an oil base, Solomon took almost all the oil out of his paints: the oil colors were placed on soft paper, and most of the oil was absorbed as a result. These colors were then re-activated with mineral spirits and carefully wiped on with a cloth or scrubbed over the surface with a brush.

Final varnishing was completed on a sunny day. Beeswax was shaved into a double boiler and melted. *Liquitex* Polymer Medium was poured into the wax and slightly warmed. This special varnish was sprayed on the sun-warmed painting. (A mouth atomizer or flit gun can be used for spraying warm varnish.) Solomon says this process reduces bubbles and "bloom."

Color Plate 14. FORM A EXPAND, 20×18 inches, by Russell Woody, 1963. Media: *Liquitex* and ink.

In this example of a work using ink with *Liquitex* in a mixed media application, heavy cotton duck canvas was stretched and given two coats of gesso. All line was drawn on the gesso ground in India ink with a reed pen, a stick, and a quill pen. (Such a surface is an excellent one for drawings. The texture of the canvas may be varied for unusual effects.)

A varnish of gloss medium was quickly brushed over the ink lines. Multiple glazes followed. Some of the glazes were worked wet-into-wet, as in the watercolor technique. The final painting was given a gloss varnish.

The work was based on a development of forms related, in part, to a painting by Veronese.

Color Plate 15. EXCURSION, 120×210 inches, by Robert Goodnough, 1963. Media: *Liquitex, Aqua-Tec* and oil. (Courtesy: the artist.)

This photograph of *Excursion,* taken just before it was completed, shows the painting still in the process of evolutionary change. Several areas and forms are still to be refined and shifted. Shape is paramount to Goodnough, and so are the tension and conflict that arise from association of ideas. In his very personal, fluxionary painting, he continues to manipulate his shapes until a definite statement of esthetic intent has been accomplished.

Commenting on *Excursion,* Goodnough says: "Basically, it is done in a manner similar to that I have used in many of my recent paintings — starting with forms or shapes made usually with polymer emulsions and working toward oil. Often I work out the shapes with masking tape and fill in the areas with color. Many of the final shapes are in oil, so that there is an interesting contrast between the matte quality of the plastics and the oil paint surface. The fast drying is a help to the building-up process which I often use. Many of the brighter colors are the plastics in this particular painting."

The painting is on commercially primed canvas.

Chapter 8 / Textural Painting and Collage

Textural Painting. The polymer emulsions are excellent adhesives; this was in fact one of the first commercial uses of the synthetic resins. This adhesiveness can be used to advantage in the types of painting, very popular now, in which various ingredients are added to the paint or in which extraneous materials are incorporated into the surface of a painting. It is also ideal for collage.

Artists who today throw almost anything under, into, and on top of the paint film would find an answer to their many problems if they used the synthetics. The majority of them are still using oils and glues, often with disastrous results. The paintings are cracking, peeling, losing their color, and are in a general state of disrepair a few years after they were painted.

I have used textural processes in my own paintings for a number of years, striving for a tactile as well as a painterly surface. Beginning with a conception of natural form linked with implications and ideas related to that form, I work between this idea and immediate reactions to physical paint quality, the one fostering and modifying the other. I have found the synthetics an ideal medium to allow this free flow and interaction of mental idea with sensuous reaction.

As textural adjuncts to painting I have used sand, small rock, powdered fiber glass (crushed fiber insulation bats used for house insulation), glass beads, ground pastels, silicas, spackling compound, cement, dried modeling paste, marble dust, sawdust, cloths and papers of all types, powdered carborundum, and the dried plastic emulsion skins scraped from the glass palette. All these were used sparingly, and not usually in combination. Surface quality should not become a fetish, but an esthetic reaction that is somehow inherent within a specific painting.

Some of these additives—those of a granular particle nature—may be mixed with color in order to give the paint itself a particular texture. Whenever such inert particles are added to polymer emulsions, the particles must be thoroughly saturated with medium (either gloss medium or matte medium) before mixing in with the colors. Otherwise the additives will absorb the medium needed to surround and isolate the pigments, and a weak paint film will result. The detail of *Whither Goest Thou—Sixth to Ninth Hour* (Color Plates 16 and 17, page 73), shows the effect of powdered fiber glass mixed with pigments (after first having been thoroughly wet with medium). It gives a texture of fine but uneven sand and has the advantage of being lighter. It becomes part of the paint film.

Many additives may be presented in their own right rather than covered with pigment. Black carborundum, for example, has color qualities that can be shown to advantage. I used glass beads in the painting *Bullfight: Mexico* (Figure 30), a semi-allegorical study painted after my return from Mexico. As it developed it seemed too painterly —too slick—for the rather garish effect I wanted. The matador's cape especially seemed to resemble bullfight posters too much. I was renting a studio from an optometrist at the time, and came across a supply of tiny glass beads used for heating the frames of glasses. Those beads seemed to have the quality of flashy brilliance I wanted for the matador's cape—the traditional "coat of many lights." I painted polymer medium over the cape and coat and then poured the beads into the wet surface. When the medium had dried after fifteen minutes, the beads were set fast. Another coat of the gloss medium was brushed over the beads, encasing the whole in a plastic sheath.

Raymond Jonson, Professor Emeritus at the University of New Mexico, started using *Liquitex*, as well as industrial brands of plastic, in 1957 and has produced over one hundred and eighty paintings in the synthetics since that time. Throughout his career, both as artist and teacher, he has insisted on

Figure 30. BULLFIGHT: MEXICO (detail), 16×16 inches, by Russell Woody, 1961–63. Medium: *Liquitex* with glass beads.

Glass beads were cemented to a Masonite support with polymer medium to create the granular texture that can be seen on the right portion of this detail. (When placed in direct light, the beads normally produce a brilliant reflection. When a direct light is used to take a photograph of them, however, it simply creates a glare. Therefore, an oblique light had to be used to take this photo; as a result, the beads reflect only slightly.)

Clear polymer medium was first painted over the color area intended for the beads. They were then sprinkled into the medium while it was still wet. In fifteen minutes, when the medium had dried, the beads were set, and an additional coat of medium was applied over them to insure their adhesion. This coating encased the beads in a sort of plastic pocket. The beads broke the color underneath, refracting the light and producing a depth that was unexpected. Any additives may be attached to a surface in this manner to retain their special characteristics of color, reflection, or natural shapes.

The heavy texture on the left is composed of modeling paste, directly applied and painted over.

craftsmanship and permanency in art. When he used oils he applied them in the painstaking traditional manner, working from lean to fat. His paintings have changed in technique and esthetic effect as a result of adopting the polymer emulsions; and as a side result, he no longer needs to spend so much concern on craftsmanship.

Jonson has experimented with the synthetics in a wide range of techniques. In *Polymer No. 21–1958* (Figure 31), color was poured on and controlled by the forced pressure of an air brush which pushed the wet color into patterned areas. If the color began to dry at times, he sprayed it with water to restore its resiliency.

Today Jonson is fascinated with the textural additives that the polymer emulsions invite so readily. His tables are covered with bottles and cans of shaved Plexiglas, clean pine sawdust, white sand, marble dust, and ripped wood shavings. Drawers are filled with brilliant cut or poured shapes of dried polymer emulsion color, which he sometimes incorporates into paintings. (Color Plate 18, page 76). These thin sheets are made by pouring the acrylic paint on a slab of glass, soaking the sheets in water, and removing them when they detach themselves from the surface. They are placed between layers of waxed paper to keep them from sticking together (all the synthetic emulsions are pressure sensitive to a slight degree and will stick under continuous pressure). Fragments of old paint are also cut into small particles and kept in jars until Jonson decides they will benefit a particular work.

A detail of *Polymer No. 6–1963* (Figure 32) shows how black sand and redwood shavings were applied in textural contrast to the soft background color.

Collage. Collage means "pasting", and that is literally what is done in this relatively new art form. Collage had its roots in Cubism, when textures or objects were duplicated or suggested by gluing bits of the objects, or things that resembled them onto the canvas. Today, collage holds its own as a fine arts technique and is especially popular with the abstractionists and pop artists.

Either polymer medium or matte medium can be used as the gluing agent in collage, to affix paper or other collage materials to a support. The medium forms an excellent bond and protects the material in the same manner as it protects additives in textural painting.

Many artists use commercial polyvinyl or acrylic glues in collage, and these often work well. They are not recommended, however, unless the artist knows the exact chemical makeup of the glue. Chemical reactions could take place, especially if the glue is mixed with emulsion paints. Another danger even greater than mixing lies in the commercial glues themselves. They are not formulated for retention of color and may discolor. Many of them contain inferior grades of plasticizing agents, which are used to give flexibility to vinyls especially. When used in collage, some of these plasticizers migrate—that is, they move into adjacent paint layers and are absorbed by the support or evaporate, thus causing the plastic to become brittle. Therefore, the fine arts synthetic paint media are superior to commercial plastic emulsion glues for artistic purposes.

In making a collage of flat pieces of paper, each piece should be thoroughly coated with the medium and immediately applied to the support, which also has been given a brushing of the medium. The two surfaces should be pressed together while both are wet. If wrinkles or bubbles occur, the paper can be peeled up while wet and gently brushed, rolled or pressed down again. A stiff bristle brush or hard rubber roller is very handy for this purpose.

If large sheets of paper or canvas are to be used in collage, one end of the sheet should be pressed down first while the major portion is kept out of contact with the wet support. The paper or fabric can be rolled back on itself. Bit by bit it is rolled out with a brayer or carefully pressed down with the palm of the hand. To prevent edges from curling while drying, the material can be weighted with books or other heavy objects.

Rippled, crushed or wrinkled paper can also be glued to a surface. The textures dry rigid and can be painted over, if desired. Gauze, toweling, transparent

Color Plate 16. WHITHER GOEST THOU – SIXTH TO NINTH HOUR (detail), 6×8 inches, by Russell Woody, 1960. Media: *Politec* and powdered Fiberglas.

This detail shows how additives—in this case powdered Fiberglas—can be mixed with emulsion paints for unusual effects. The Fiberglas was obtained in insulating bat form and powdered by rubbing the fibers between gloved hands. The powder was then soaked in polymer medium before it was incorporated in the paint. (This prevents the additive from absorbing too much medium from the pigments and thus weakening the paint film.) The resulting mixture was brushed on in heavy strokes.

The central white form is of modeling paste that has been dragged on the Masonite support with the fingers. The sandy texture is the Fiberglas.

Glazes, washes, and scumbles of paint were used over the impasto areas.

Color Plate 17. WHITHER GOEST THOU – SIXTH TO NINTH HOUR, 72×48 inches, 1960. Media: *Politec* and powdered Fiberglas.

A detail of this painting is seen in Color Plate 16. The paint that was made matte in certain areas by the addition of Fiberglas contrasts greatly with the glazed, gloss areas.

Details of the technique used are given in the caption for Color Plate 16 and in the text.

collage—and unique ones, at that. The two that are reproduced in this book (Figures 34 and 35), both untitled, show how he has employed a wide variety of additive materials, using plastic gesso as an adhesive. Figure 34 is a detail of the latter collage. Chavatel's *Unititled* painting No. 2 (Color Plate 19, page 76) is particularly interesting in that it consists of six separate paintings brought together as a harmonious whole. Since the painting support as well as the painting surface is handled in collage technique, the result is possibly the ultimate in collage.

Simulated Stained Glass Collage. The polymer emulsions can be used to make mock stained glass windows, or freestanding translucent colored screens. This technique is based on the ability of the medium to be easily stripped up from glass, plastic wrap, or oily surfaces. Emulsion colors are mixed with a large quantity of polymer medium—the amount of medium depending on the degree of transparency desired. This mixture is poured onto the horizontal non-absorbent surface, allowed to dry, soaked in water, and removed. The shapes can be controlled by surrounding the area to be poured with an oil-base modeling clay. The thickness of the pieces can also be controlled in this manner. Of course large areas can be poured and cut to shape.

The polymer pieces are then collaged together by placing the shapes about one-quarter or one-eighth inch apart on the non-absorbent surface and filling the "lines" between with clear or colored medium. When the connecting lines are dry, these simulated stained glass works can then be clamped between panes of glass or sheets of hard plastic with metal strips or clamps and hung or set into position.

Such plastic pieces can also be used in mobiles and back-lighted bas relief panels. Many glazes can be employed in this process, as well as painting manipulations, so that the effects of the panels can be endless and quite unusual. Also objects, such as leaves, grasses, butterflies, etc. (the list can be endless), can be embedded in, or between, poured clear plastic layers.

It must be remembered that the plastics are pliable, not rigid on drying. They require some sort of stiff, transparent backing to obtain rigidity.

A unique collage painting process may be achieved by using only these multiple transparencies adhered with polymer medium one over the other on a painting support.

Color Plate 18. POLYMER NO. 45-1962, 18×24 inches, by Raymond Jonson, 1962. Medium: *Liquitex* collage. (Courtesy: the artist.)

When polymer emulsions dry on a hard, shiny surface such as glass or metal, they can easily be removed by wetting the dried plastic film and peeling it off. Such films were the basis for this completely plastic collage by Raymond Jonson.

The translucent forms on the lower left and the circular forms which run between the two large black areas are *Liquitex* paint films that were stripped from the tops of the bottles in which the colors are sold. Jonson affixed the dry plastic skins—which most artists usually discard—to the paper support with polymer medium.

The artist then created similar films for the large black shapes and the red within them by pouring *Liquitex* colors on glass. To achieve the runs, he tilted the glass; to produce the rings, he pulled wet paint out and looped it around with a stick. When the plastic had dried, he wetted it and removed it from the glass. Polymer Medium was used to glue the forms to the paper.

Jonson keeps sheets of these poured plastic films in his studio for collage purposes. They are stored between pieces of wax paper. Old paint which looks like plastic confetti and can also be used in collage techniques, is scraped from the palette, cut into small shapes and placed in jars.

Color Plate 19. UNTITLED painting No. 2, 48×12 inches, by George Chavatel, 1963. Medium: *Liquitex* collage. (Courtesy: the artist.)

A unique collage indeed is this one by George Chavatel. The artist has the following to say about it:

"The most recent use I have had for the acrylic emulsion *Liquitex* was related to a personal problem which should be of interest to those whose concern is a physical alteration in the normal flatness of the two-dimensional painting surface. To achieve such an alteration—to create a variegated physical surface and make possible as many projections and recessions as I wanted—I decided in this case to break the painting surface into eight separate projective and recessive Masonite panels, each measuring twelve inches in height, one-fourth inch in thickness. They ranged from two to nine inches in width.

"Upon these eight panels were affixed pieces of cardboard, sawdust and wood shavings, sand, crushed egg shells, and *Liquitex* Modeling Paste. These additional materials were integrated physically and visually into the three-dimensional setting in such a way as to counter other elements within the design scheme, yet still relate to the whole."

Modeling paste was used to enhance the surfaces of some of the projected forms, and *Liquitex* Polymer Medium was used as an adhesive for attaching the additive materials and as a protective varnish over the entire four-foot surface

Color Plate 20. COLLAGE 1963, 22×28 inches, Nicholas Krushenik, 1963. Medium: *Liquitex* collage. (Courtesy: the artist.)

Nicholas Krushenik makes brilliantly colored collage paper with *Liquitex*. He adds a small amount of water to the paints, applies them to sheets of rag paper, then cuts the paper into shapes. These are stapled to another large white piece of paper. In this collage, note that where the paper is not stapled, as toward the center, shadows lend another quality to the work, establishing a type of depth.

Krushenik paints paper rather than using colored papers because he does not think that any colored papers he has seen have the quality or intensity of color inherent in the plastic colors.

Figure 34. UNTITLED painting No. 1, 12×12 inches, by George Chavatel, 1962. Media: *Liquitex* Gesso collage with oil glazes. (Courtesy: the artist.)

In this painting by George Chavatel, *Liquitex* Gesso was used both as a binding medium for textural additives and as a ground. Very thin oil glazes were applied over the gesso base for color and to emphasize surface quality.

As Chavatel describes his painting process: "*Liquitex* Gesso was applied to a surface of the canvas, which had been glued with a casein adhesive to a panel of plywood, a quarter-inch thick and twelve inches square.

"While the third coat was wet, facial tissue, gauze, and pulp paper (hand-towel variety) were applied to this moist gesso coating. Another heavy application was applied over the additive materials while they—as well as the previous coating—were still moist. After all four gesso coatings were sufficiently dry, two further thin coats were applied to the entire surface. One of these covering coats was slightly diluted with water to avoid excessive build-up of gesso areas, which might have affected the desired projection of the additive materials.

"Upon waiting out the drying period, which took only a few hours, I applied an oil glaze mixture of nine parts turpentine, nine parts damar varnish, two parts Venice turpentine, and two parts stand oil to the entire surface. This vehicle contained green, blue, and black oil color. Almost immediately I wiped away this glaze to expose the subtleties of the additive projections as well as allow the opulence of the *Liquitex* Gesso to be seen through the tinting color over it.

"The versatility of the synthetic gesso produced a fusion of surface and textural supplements and provided a union that was not only durable but esthetically pleasing. As far as I'm concerned, this gesso has proved to be superior to, or at least more reliable than, any other ground material."

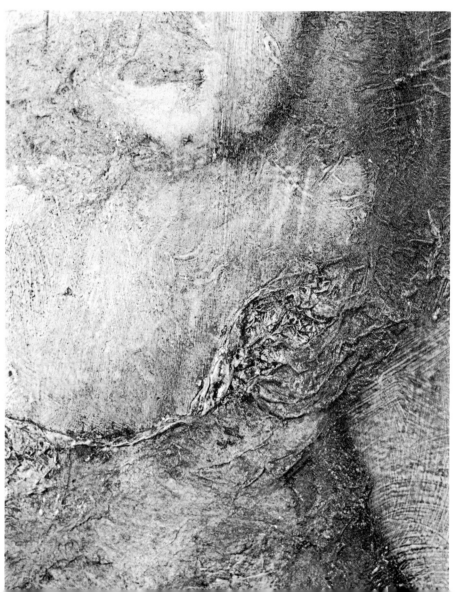

Figure 35. UNTITLED painting No. 1 (detail), 3×2½ inches, by George Chavatel, 1962. Media: *Liquitex* Gesso collage with oil glazes. (Courtesy: the artist.)

This is a detail of Figure 34 showing the use of paper toweling as a permanent textural collage surface. On top of, and covered with, synthetic gesso, this section could easily be produced in a three-foot format as well as in one of three inches. It would still have the same qualities of texture emphasis and permanency.

Chapter 9 / As a Mural Medium

Mural decoration can easily be accomplished with the polymer emulsions. The synthetics can be painted directly over mural grounds such as concrete, plaster, and even concrete block. The paints do not sink in but stay on the surface of all porous materials with remarkable adhesion. The only requirement is that the wall surface be clean and free of loose particles. Any amount of impasto can be applied, as in easel painting. Even metal strips and ceramic pieces may be sealed into the surface. When this is done, the metal must have a roughened or pitted surface (such as anodized aluminum which can be "anodized" by being placed in caustic soda for a few minutes, thus "etching" the surface), and the ceramic must be unglazed.

The best support for mural painting is a false wall erected in front of an existing wall. The use of a false wall eliminates the dangers inherent in the expansion and contraction of a plaster wall. It also protects against cracking or peeling plaster and damage to masonry walls by water seepage from behind.

Untempered Masonite panels have proved most useful as false walls. They should be fastened securely to a wood frame backing with the Masonite glued to cross bracings at least every twenty-four inches, using top grade furniture,

animal glue. The backs of these should be sealed with an acrylic resin or acrylic lacquer to prevent warping. Large murals may need several sheets of Masonite. If so, a space of one-eighth to one-quarter inch should be left between panels when putting them together. A piece of linen spanning this gap and glued to the Masonite with a polymer medium keeps the wall continuous. If there are bumps or lines where butting occurs, five or six coats of gesso or Titanium White as a ground will obliterate them. If a canvas support is desired, it can be glued to the Masonite with a polymer medium.

The mechanical technique of mural painting is the same as painting any other surface. Water, however, should not be used for thinning paints for mural use; the clear emulsion, either matte or gloss should be used for thinning purposes because it will create a stronger and more durable film. On all absorbent surfaces, use gesso or the emulsion medium as a ground to insure a smooth flow of paint.

After a mural is completed, a varnish coating of polymer medium or matte varnish should be applied to protect the paint. If the mural is outdoors and exposed to weather, another varnish of acrylic resin (as opposed to an emulsified acrylic or vinyl) would be advisable (see Part III, Chapter 1 for

resins suitable for this purpose). No paint existing today will stand direct weather exposure for a long period of time. All organic materials, as well as inorganic matter, are eventually affected by the sun and constant weathering by the elements. However, if a coating of resin is applied every year or two, a polymer mural should last for a long time. The *Liquitex* manufacturer has had a small test mural facing south and exposed to all weather conditions, including rain and snow, for seven years. In three years it began to show the eroding effects of weather — the more transparent passages weathering much faster due to greater penetration of the paint film by ultraviolet rays. A traditional paint would have vanished long before under such abuse.

Independence and the Opening of the West (Figure 36) is a mural painted by Thomas Hart Benton for the Harry S. Truman Library in Independence, Missouri. Its unique appearance results from Benton's strongly three-dimensional style of painting in combination with the brilliant and luminous quality of the plastic medium. Benton made many studies and sketches before starting the work, and he also constructed a three-dimensional clay model in high detail which he could study for light and shadow values (see Figure 37). Benton started making clay models for

Figure 36. INDEPENDENCE AND THE OPENING OF THE WEST, mural 19×32 feet, by Thomas Hart Benton, 1961. Medium: *Liquitex*. (Courtesy: Harry S. Truman Library.)

While a traditional tempera technique was used to execute this mural, the medium employed was a synthetic polymer, *Liquitex*. Thinned with water, it emulates the traditional medium almost exactly. Thomas Hart Benton was one of the first to exploit the plastic tempera mural possibilities to their fullest.

The colors of the mural are rich and unusually brilliant. It would have been difficult, if not impossible, to achieve this brilliancy with any of the traditional paints.

This is the technical story of the development of the mural:

The wall was supported with steel mesh and plastered. A plastic sealer was painted over the original plaster paint to prevent later bleeding of that paint. A heavy Belgian linen was then attached to the wall with polyester adhesive. When six coats of full-strength *Liquitex* Gesso had been given the linen as a ground, the prepared wall was squared off in three-quarter-inch squares, and the cartoon for the mural was transferred, in pencil, in the traditional manner. Thinned *Liquitex* was applied in a direct tempera technique over the pencil design. Painting ran from coarse brush work done with large bristle brushes at the top to detailed work done with small sable brushes at eye-level.

Since the mural faces large windows, reflection from these could have destroyed the effectiveness of the work. Therefore, the mural was given a final matte varnish. As can be seen in this reproduction, no reflection is evident on the mural, although there are glares on the surface of the floor and the marble wall.

Benton's actual painting time was eight months. However, he had spent many months doing extensive preparatory work beforehand. The mural was completed in 1961 and dedicated on the artist's seventy-second birthday.

many of his works in 1919 when he read that Tintoretto used this device. Unfortunately the original model for the Truman Library mural was destroyed when a sculptor tried to cast it in bronze.

The 495-square-foot mural was painted on heavy Belgian linen attached with polyester adhesive to a plaster wall reenforced with steel mesh. Six coats of full strength gesso were used as ground. Benton used a standard tempera technique in executing the mural. He transferred a cartoon to the squared-off canvas in the traditional manner. Over this pencil design, he applied *Liquitex* paint. In order to aid the eye of the viewer on such a large work, Benton painted the upper area in a relatively free and broad manner, using large bristle brushes, and developed the lower areas at eye level with finely detailed work accomplished with small sable brushes (Figure 38 shows this broad kind of manipulation).

Many other artists have used plastic emulsions for murals, too. Garo Antreasian, artist in residence at Indiana

Figure 37. Three-dimensional study for INDEPENDENCE AND THE OPENING OF THE WEST, 22×42 inches, by Thomas Hart Benton. Media: Clay model painted with *Liquitex* egg tempera. (Courtesy: Harry S. Truman Library.)

Thomas Hart Benton often builds three-dimensional models to study the ways in which light falls on figures and objects and how it affects color. He began to build such models in 1919 when he read that it was a practice of Tintoretto. It is especially adaptable to Benton's manner, because he is greatly concerned with space (as he says, "I think in three dimensions").

Because of the size of the work to be done, this clay study is more detailed than most of Benton's three-dimensional sketches. He does not copy from them, but simply uses the models as a point of departure. They are directly built up with modeling clay, and then painted with traditional egg tempera or with Benton's own mixture of egg yolk and *Liquitex*—a mixture which both duplicates the traditional medium in visual quality and provides a more permanent and versatile paint.

When I visited Benton in his studio home in Martha's Vineyard not so long ago, he was working on an easel painting with egg yolk mixed with *Liquitex* colors and media. Behind him was one of his models—a three-dimensional build-up of the painting on which he was working. Parts of it were very "unfinished," but it had served its purpose as an exacting study and point of departure.

Figure 38. INDEPENDENCE AND THE OPENING OF THE WEST (detail), by Thomas Hart Benton. Medium: *Liquitex*. (Courtesy: Harry S. Truman Library.)

This is a detail of the top center portion of the mural *Independence and the Opening of the West*, described in the caption for Figure 36. It shows the broad handling Benton used in these upper sections, as opposed to the fine detail at eye-level. Although the brush strokes are broad and loosely applied, the artist's control is exact.

If precise detail had been used throughout, the viewer would have trouble seeing the work as a unified design—the detail causing his eyes to strain in focusing on the uppermost areas. Benton's technique helps the eye compensate for both distance and viewing angle.

Color Plate 21. THE ELEMENTS, mural 12 feet × 6 feet 4 inches (composed of three panels, each 48×76 inches), by Leo Manso, 1961. Medium: *Liquitex*. (Collection: Lincoln Public Library, Lincoln, Nebraska.)

An example of an abstract mural done with *Liquitex* this work by Leo Manso was painted on one-half-inch-thick Masonite panels. Each of the three panels was cradled with one-by-three-inch pine strips attached to the panel under pressure with Elmer's Glue. A three-coat ground of *Liquitex* Gesso was applied. Each coat was sanded smooth. *Liquitex* colors, thinned with water, were used. Matte medium was employed in glazing, and modeling paste and sand were used for heavy impastos.

"This mural evolved organically from thin to thick, or heavy, painting," Manso says. "There was no planning of the artistic concept; rather, the theme was a continuation of a body of work concerned with light, erosion, movement, earth.

"A panel was started, carried to a middle stage of finish, then set aside. A second panel was begun and brought to a higher level of finish. The first panel was placed in the central position, and the second one placed to the left. These were further integrated. The last panel was resolved rather fully and placed to the right.

"All three panels were then worked on all over to bring the work into a conceptual and artistic unity.

"Technically, painting was begun with the panels placed flat on waist-high stools. This made for the greatest freedom in painting, since it permitted walking around the work in any direction. The panels were later laid against a wall so they could be seen in a vertical position.

"Transparent washes of *Liquitex* pigment, water, and matte medium started the painting. Corrections, or deletions, were made with *Liquitex* Gesso over unsatisfactory areas. The painting was then built, in part, into thick areas, with modeling paste used for impasto and color and medium added. Sometimes indications drawn in pastel colors were sprayed with the matte medium to bind them. Later, for extremely dense areas, more paste, pigment, sand, and additional binder were applied.

"Where luminosity was desired, *Liquitex* Gesso with binder was applied, and glazes of transparent color laid over the clear under-painted white.

"When the panels were finished they were locked into position with metal straps screwed into the back of the wood cradling."

University, painted a 1080-square-foot *Liquitex* mural at the university (see Figure 39). It was painted on canvas cemented to backing. Antreasian estimates that he reduces his painting time by 30 per cent in using the fast drying polymer emulsions. This is the oldest mural painted in *Liquitex*, and it was for this mural that *Liquitex* was developed.

A panoramic sweep of Vermont life past and present was painted by Paul Sample for National Life Insurance Company in Montpelier (Figure 40). It is fifty feet long by eight feet high.

The decorative murals of Douglas Riseborough are based on the Venetian style of painting. He first draws the design on canvas in a freehand sketch. Then all figures and objects are painted one by one in the tempera manner. Figure 41 is a portion of a mural done for a Los Angeles residence.

Polymer emulsions are as successful in producing abstract murals as they are for realistic techniques or decorative, manneristic interpretations. Leo Manso's *The Elements* (Color Plate 21, opposite) in the Lincoln Public Library, Lincoln, Nebraska, is an excellent example of an abstract mural in plastic. Its surfaces range from transparent and luminous areas to dense, opaque, and heavily textured effects. Although the concepts were not created specifically or literally, the artist was concerned with the basic ideas of light, erosion, movement, and earth.

Manso painted *The Elements* on three Masonite panels, each four feet by six feet four inches, which were given three coats of gesso. The three panels were painted individually and together, horizontally and vertically. Modeling paste, polymer medium, and sand were used as well as polymer emulsion colors to give textural variety. If certain areas became unsatisfactory during the course of the painting, or if a greater degree of transparency was desired in a certain glaze, Manso re-established grounds with gesso and painted over it.

Manso, who teaches in Provincetown, Massachusetts, and New York City, is one of the few artist-teachers who have investigated the whole range of plastic media in their own work and instruct their students in the techniques of the synthetics.

Figure 39. HISTORY OF INDIANA UNIVERSITY, mural 6×30 feet, by Garo Z. Antreasian, 1957. Medium: *Liquitex*. (Courtesy: the artist.)

This is one of six panels, each thirty feet long, forming a mural in the men's quadrangle dining hall at Indiana University. One of the first large murals to be completed in *Liquitex*, it depicts the entire story of the University since its founding in 1920. Sixteen quarts of color were needed to cover a total of 1820 square feet. The mural includes 110 figures, of which only thirteen are seen in this panel.

Antreasian says that the medium reduced his usual painting time by thirty per cent because of its handling qualities—much faster and simpler than those of traditional mural media. The method of application was very direct and similar in manipulation to that employed for tempera.

The panels were painted on canvas cemented to backing.

Figure 40. HERITAGE OF THE HILLS (mural detail), 8×12 feet (mural size 8 × 50 feet), by Paul Sample, 1959–61. Medium: *Liquitex*. (Courtesy: National Life Insurance Company, Montpelier, Vermont.)

Heritage of the Hills, a mural painted for the National Life Insurance Company, Montpelier, Vermont, depicts the history of the area. Two canvas sections, each eight feet by twenty-five feet, were given several coats of gesso. These were painted in the artist's studio and later erected in the insurance company's main building. The method of handling was similar to that used with tempera. No final varnish was deemed necessary. The artist wanted the brilliant colors to remain completely matte.

The detail reproduced here shows agricultural, educational, spiritual, and recreational aspects of the state.

Figure 41. MOROCCO (mural detail), 48×36 inches, by H. D. Riseborough, 1961. Medium: *Liquitex*. (Courtesy: the artist.)

This detail of a mural painted for a private home shows how the polymer emulsions can be applied in decorative mural painting based on a Venetian style and technique. The support was canvas with a gesso ground. The design was drawn freehand from a preliminary sketch (the original rough was postcard-size). Objects and figures were then painted one by one. Each was completed before the next was considered, the over-all design being controlled by the sketch. Paint was applied in a direct tempera-or fresco-like manner, in which individual brush strokes show and there is little blending of colors for modeling.

Chapter 10 / Printing Techniques

The polymer emulsion media can be used in various ways to create plates from which prints may be made. Because of their impervious hardness when dry, the synthetic plates are often as durable as traditional plates of metal, wood, linoleum, and the like, and are less expensive. They also permit corrections to be made during the etching, burning or engraving process of creating the design.

Gesso Techniques. One way to prepare a synthetic plate is first to give a piece of Masonite, cut to the desired size, four or more coats of gesso which are sanded smooth. Then, six or more applications of matte medium to finish the plate's surface. The medium should be brushed on smoothly with a soft brush and thinned with water if brush marks occur (the brush textures may of course be retained if such an effect is desired). An ordinary woodburning tool is used to make incised lines in the plate; the lines will have a quality similar to those of an etching. Corrections can be made by painting over with the medium and tooling again. If the tool becomes gummy, a brand of polymer emulsion remover or lacquer thinner will clean it. (Never clean a warm burning tool with removers—the tool must be *cold*.) Drypoint characteristics can be achieved by scratching into the plate

with an etching needle (old steel phonograph needles work well if they can be found). The dry point produces a soft, sometimes fuzzy line, which may be used in combination with the burnt line if desired.

For printing, the plate is inked and its top surface wiped clean, with ink remaining in the lines. The plate can then be placed in an etching press and a slightly damp printing paper placed over it. For small work a hand press may be used. If a regulation press is not available, an old roller from a washing machine wringer can substitute. The plate can be slightly heated when using an oil base printing ink to achieve better impressions in the usual printing manner, but if this is done the number of prints is drastically reduced because the polymer will become sticky after a short period.

Papers for printing are left to the discretion of the artist. Traditional rice papers and watercolor papers make excellent prints. I have seen newsprint and pastel papers used to excellent effect. The papers should always be damp, but not wet, and there should be several inches to spare on all sides of the print.

Modeling Paste Techniques. Modeling paste, too, can be used as a surface for print making. Four or five layers of paste

paste are troweled onto a Masonite board with a palette knife. Allow each coat to dry before applying another. A total application one-eighth inch thick should be sufficient, and in any case it should not be more than one-fourth inch thick or it may crack. Each succeeding coat need not be sanded, but the last layer should be sanded level and very smooth. The paste can then be carved with engraving tools or gouges in the manner of wood engraving. Very fine and delicate lines can be achieved. To correct mistakes, paste is merely applied to any miscuts, allowed to dry, sanded and retooled. Printing is done in the wood block method: ink is rolled on with a brayer, paper placed over the plate, and pressure applied with a press or by rubbing with a spoon. Because this method is inexpensive, fast, easy to learn and equally easy to correct, it lends itself especially to school use.

Collagraphy. A relatively new printing process called *collagraphy* has been employed recently by many artists. It is a combination of collage and printing: the printing surface is not incised or molded, but constructed in a collage manner and using many collage materials such as papers and textiles.

Artist George Chavatel, now teaching at Longwood College in Farmville,

Virginia, has done considerable experimenting with collagraphy. After early trials with cardboard as a base, he now uses one-eighth-inch-thick Masonite for a more durable structure. The Masonite is sanded and its edges beveled to avoid damaging the rag stock paper on which prints are to be made.

Chavatel uses two different techniques in collagraphy. In the first process, he applies a coating of polymer medium to the Masonite and, while it is wet, he adds the textural materials. Another coating of medium is quickly applied over the additives so that the two moist coatings of plastic will harden simultaneously, solidly encasing the additives. Two final coatings of polymer medium insure adhesion of the affixed materials (see Figure 42).

Materials which Chavatel finds most satisfying for collagraphy include pelon, paper towels, gauze, and netting (tulle-like mesh). Also, in order to get varying textural effects, he grinds various powders and granular materials into polymer medium and brushes them on the plate—either above or below the collage materials. Some typical additives are silicon carbide abrasive powders, grinding quartz used for grinding lithograph stones, sand, and modeling paste. Sensitive handling of these various textures can achieve great richness and variety in tonal surface, which is well transmitted to paper.

In Chavatel's second collagraphy technique, he first applies gesso to the Masonite sheet in three to six coatings. (Figures 43 and 44 are examples of this second method.) The gesso is not sanded, because sanding would destroy the textural quality the gesso gives. This textural ground handsomely supplements the textures which are then brushed on—silicon carbide, grinding quartz, and modeling paste each mixed with polymer medium. As many as six protective coatings of polymer medium protect the individual qualities of tone and texture even after many printings.

Inking and printing of the collagraphy plates is done in the traditional manner. Chavatel uses cold press drawing and watercolor papers in grades ranging from sixty-five to two hundred pounds. Inks are very easily wiped off

Figure 42. UNTITLED Collagraphy Print, 18×18 inches, by George Chavatel, 1962. Medium: *Liquitex* with textural additives. (Courtesy: the artist.)

This collagraphy was printed from a Masonite plate which had been given several coats of gesso for a brushed texture. Cardboard shapes were attached to the gesso ground with polymer medium to achieve the vertical patterns to the left and the very dark areas were done with carborundum particles attached in the same manner. Gesso was heavily applied to effect the curved textural lines.

The print was made on a heavy watercolor paper with press adjusted to almost maximum pressure so that the paper became almost incised with the textural design.

Figure 43. UNTITLED Collagraphy Print, 12×12 inches, by George Chavatel, 1962. Medium: *Liquitex* with textural additives. (Courtesy: the artist.)

Collagraphy is a combination of collage and printing—the printing surface being built up in a collage manner. George Chavatel, who has experimented widely with this process, made this print as follows:

A one-eighth-inch-thick Masonite panel was cut to twelve by twelve inches, sanded, and its edges beveled. Four coats of *Liquitex* Gesso were applied to complete the basic plate.

Silicon carbide and grinding quartz was mixed with *Liquitex* Polymer Medium and brushed onto the gesso surface to create a granular texture. (The rich tonal effects were produced by these abrasives.) To prevent these additives from cutting the printing paper and to insure their adhesion, five coats of medium were applied over them.

The surface was then given another coat of the medium, and paper hand towels, gauze, tulle netting, and strips of cloth were affixed while the surface was wet. Still another coat of medium bound the materials in place. (The towels created the relief-like impression; the different types of cloth over the other textures established the strong directional shapes.)

The inking and printing of the final collage plate was accomplished in the traditional printing manner. It is very easy to wipe ink from the untextured surface areas of such a plate because of the protective coats of medium.

Collagraphy processes offer a more varied means of textural printing than any other traditional means; mezzotint, aquatint, and etched and incised line effects may also be achieved by collagraphy. It is one of the least expensive printing processes.

Figure 44. UNTITLED Collagraphy Print (detail), 4×3½ inches, by George Chavatel, 1962. Medium: *Liquitex* with textural additives. (Courtesy: the artist.)

This is a detail of Figure 43 showing the lower right section of the collagraphy print. The tulle netting creates almost the effect of wire. Most of the textures result from paper toweling and cloth having been sealed to the plate with *Liquitex* Medium. A piece of gauze made the impression seen at upper left.

the untextured surface areas. To protect the plate, polymer medium should be applied on the back and edges of the plate, as well as the front; this acts as a seal against moisture absorption.

Interesting linear patterns may be achieved in collagraphs by the incising of lines into the multiple layers of the polymer medium with an ordinary woodburning tool. The lines provide a contrast to the predominate areas of tone, as well as serving to define certain tonal masses.

Monoprints. Monoprints are made by painting with polymer emulsion color on a sheet of glass or other hard, nonporous surface and, while the paint is wet, placing paper over the painting to transfer the design. A more interesting print, on the order of serigraphy, can be achieved by transferring several prints, one on top of the other. Transparent washes of color can be overlaid indefinitely. Opaques for surface definition or underneath transparents vary the techniques.

Silk Screen Blockout and Printing Inks. The polymer emulsion mediums may be used as an excellent silk screen blockout liquid. Either the clear or tinted (for clarity) mediums (matte or gloss) may be painted onto the silk and allowed to dry. Water-base printing inks can be squeegeed over the polymer blockout. The tubed, viscous polymer emulsion colors can also be used for an ink when slightly diluted with medium. Printing must be done quickly and continuously in order that the paints do not dry on the silk. Cloth, silk screened with the emulsion paints, can be washed according to directions for washing synthetic fabrics.

Chapter 11 / Use as a Sculptural Medium

The synthetic media may be used in several sculptural techniques. The most immediate is the use of modeling paste direct from the can.

Remove the paste from the container and allow water to evaporate until the paste reaches the consistency of modeling clay. The paste must be "cured" like clay to prevent cracking and hardening of the surface. Work in gel medium in a ratio of about one part gel to two parts paste to prevent cracking. Direct modeling with the hands can then be done. (Applying cold cream to the hands will help in removing the paste when cleaning up.) When the piece dries further, it can be carved with a knife or other tool; it usually takes a day before this stage of work may progress. After four or five days the work is hard enough to be chiseled, sanded, filed, or buffed. In its natural state, the modeling paste sculpture looks like plaster. Polishing or filing gives it the character of white marble. Dried forms of modeling paste are very tough and will withstand considerable shock. They may literally be bounced on the floor (if there are no delicate projections).

While the paste is wet, polymer colors can be mixed in, to resemble any natural colored rock or wood, for example. The sculpture may also be painted when dry. Before painting, the piece should first be sealed over with polymer medium. The medium should also be mixed with colors for painting. A patina similar to metal can be obtained by rubbing on types of gilt such as *Treasure Gold, Copper,* etc.

In larger scaled works, inner base forms may be used to reduce the amount of paste needed, thus minimizing cost as well as reducing weight. These forms may be made of Styrofoam, wood, papier-mâché, Perlite, or Vermiculite. Styrofoam and wood should be cut to approximate shapes and given a coat of polymer medium. Shredded paper, sawdust, Perlite, and Vermiculite should be mixed with one-half water and one-half polymer medium and molded into shape and allowed to dry before paste is added. Modeling paste is then applied over the base form and may be molded or carved as previously described (see Figure 45).

Successive layers of modeling paste may be added to a sculpture at any time; they form a complete physical bond with preceding layers. If the sculpture is completely dry, however, it must be redampened before a new layer is applied. This will prevent the dry area from absorbing the binder from the newly attached piece, thus causing the piece to crack from too rapid a rate of water evaporation.

As a Glaze for Clay. A gloss polymer medium will give unfired clay work the brilliancy and gloss of fired clay glazes. This technique of creating unfired clay glazes is especially suitable for chil-dren's work and classroom studies when limited time or money prevents the use of fired glazes.

Polymer Cement. Polymer cement sculptural techniques are described in Chapter 15.

Repairing Sculptures. Modeling paste can be used to repair sculptures in wood, plaster, stone, and cement in such a realistic manner that the synthetic medium cannot be detected. Frederic Taubes has restored numerous icons and sculptures from all periods of art history with modeling paste. The viewer usually cannot distinguish between the original and the restored areas. (Figures 46, 47 and 48 are examples of Taubes' restorations.)

Frame Decoration. Gesso and modeling paste can be used in various ways to create very elegant frames in a very inexpensive manner. The gesso is an excellent ground for gilding, and it can be combed while wet to achieve textural and wood-grain simulations. The modeling paste can be manipulated into rococo patterns or rope and bead ornamentations. It can be stroked and textured with palette knives, combs, or broken razors. Figures may be carved into the paste when it dries, or it can be modeled with the hands when wet. (Figures 49 and 50 illustrate some frame possibilities.)

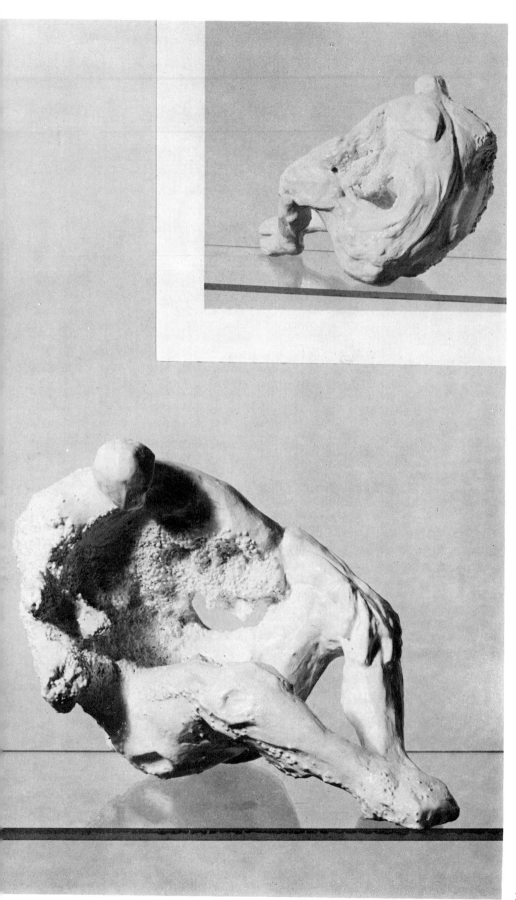

Figure 45. UNTITLED Sculpture, 12 inches high, by Russell Woody, 1964. Medium: *Liquitex* Modeling Paste.

This polymer emulsion sculpture was built on a base form of papier-mâché—the paper mixed with polymer medium. When the base was dry, a mixture of modeling paste and gel medium was applied in several layers. This was carved, shaped with a rasp and sanded smooth. Gravel was applied with polymer medium to achieve the rough, textural areas. The whole piece was given two coats of Titanium White and polymer medium as a finish.

Figure 46. Restored Gothic head (14th century). Medium: *Liquitex* Modeling Paste. (Courtesy: Frederic Taubes.)

So effectively can sculptures be restored with *Liquitex* Modeling Paste that the restored areas are not distinguishable by the naked eye.

Here the dotted areas show the restored sections. These sections were eaten away by worms (the head is solid walnut). The damage had to be removed and replaced with modeling paste mixed with powdered umber pigment. This gave the correct color to the paste and made it stiff. A magnifying glass has to be used to discover the joints of the added areas.

The restoration was done by artist Frederic Taubes, whose studio in Haverstraw, New York, is filled with classical objects which he has restored. He has duplicated various wood, stone, and even marble figures with modeling paste.

FIGURE 45

90

FIGURE 46

FIGURE 47

FIGURE 48

Figures 47 and 48. Restored angel head with wings (15th century). Medium: *Liquitex* Modeling Paste. (Courtesy: Frederic Taubes.)

Frederic Taubes has used *Liquitex* Modeling Paste to restore many historic icons and sculpture pieces. This fifteenth century piece lacked part of its right wing when it was purchased. The dotted line (Figure 47) indicates the restored section. A photo taken from the back (Figure 48) shows the base used to support the paste.

A section of plywood one-eighth-inch thick was cut to the general wing shape and attached to the existing section of wing. Modeling paste was mixed with umber to duplicate the figure's coloring. The paste was applied to the plywood and modeled with the hands to resemble the handling of the original. Imperfections, as seen in the major portion of the wooden figure, were also duplicated.

91

Figure 49. Frame designed by Frederic Taubes. Medium: *Liquitex* Gesso. (Photo: Richard Weede.)

This is a standard, inexpensive frame which has been decorated with tinted *Liquitex* Gesso. The gesso was painted onto the concave portion of the frame. While the gesso was wet, a notched razor blade was stroked across it to produce uneven textural patterns and contrasting color. Then an insert was added to the inside of the basic frame. The beveled edges of the insert and the border of the frame were both given a smooth coat of gesso and then gilded. The gesso makes an excellent base for gilding.

Artist Donald Pierce used this frame to complement one of his abstractions.

Figure 50. Frame designed by Frederic Taubes. Medium: *Liquitex* Gesso. (Photo: Richard Weede.)

This molding, bordered by a gilded rope pattern, was given a coat of gesso and "combed" with a palette knife while wet to produce the textured lines. The crests of the lines were then gilded. Grey gesso was used to finish the one-and-a-half-inch insert.

Chapter 12 / Commercial Art Techniques

Many commercial artists have adopted the polymer emulsions for their work, and they especially acclaim the rapid drying time of the synthetic media. A magazine illustration, for example, may be completed in a day instead of a week and sent out for reproduction ten minutes after it is finished. All the techniques outlined in this book are applicable to commercial art work. This chapter will describe a few special techniques that have been developed by some outstanding commercial artists.

Boris Artzybasheff, perhaps most widely known for his *Time* covers and humanized machines, is an exceptional craftsman who is constantly experimenting with new visual effects; his studio walls are covered with these experiments. He usually begins a work by making a detailed drawing. When working in portraiture, the drawing is often done in silverpoint on a Titanium White emulsion ground. The original drawing is then transferred to the final support by tracing the drawing over carbon paper with an old-fashioned straight phonograph needle in a holder. He uses Carter's carbon paper for electric typewriters; he discovered years ago that this midnight carbon did not fade even in sunlight, and its lines can be easily erased with a piece of cotton dipped in lighter fluid.

Most of Artzybasheff's illustrations are painted on hot pressed Whatman illustration board. Sometimes, however, he uses Masonite, to which he applies sprays of black and white paints to achieve an optical gray of about 50 per cent; he occasionally prefers the quality of semi-absorbency that such a ground gives when painted over. This gray ground is achieved by first spraying on three or four coats of *Liquitex* Mars Black, followed by a spray of a mixed white. His white is a unique formulation achieved by mixing polyvinyl acetate medium (see Chapter 15) with *Winsor and Newton* Permanent White. He also uses this white in painting.

The color applications are usually begun with transparent washes of watercolor mixed with *Liquitex* colors or polyvinyl acetate emulsions. Color is then built up from an array of media he keeps at hand—though not all are necessarily incorporated in a single work: casein, designers' colors, polymer emulsion colors and media, polyvinyl acetate, and dry pigments. Polymer glazes are often used in final phases. A final spray of water-diluted medium completes the work.

Artzybasheff works in many ways and follows no set pattern. Through his years of experimentation, he has achieved a "second nature" knowledge of his materials and knows instinctively what media and what technique will solve a problem at hand. Figure 51 and Color Plate 22, page 99, are examples of processes used to arrive at particular results.

Artist Robert Weaver used egg tempera for commercial work before he discovered the plastics. With the synthetic emulsions he could achieve the fast drying characteristics of tempera, yet could manipulate the paints more freely, in the manner of oils. Since he started using polymers he began to emphasize its similarities with the oil medium. He began to build up areas in impasto to get away from the thinner tempera quality. He became enamored with the lush, almost relief effects that he could achieve with modeling paste, and sometimes used it to extreme degrees when relevant to the illustration, as in the *Esquire* illustration (Figure 52).

Weaver has developed a very fast method of painting. He first builds a work in black, white, and grays, to establish the tonal values of the painting. (A similar technique is used by artist Bill Berry, as illustrated in Figure 53.) For a picture that is to be reproduced photographically, these tonal values are of far greater importance than finished art work. Three or four color washes complete the illus-

Figure 51. CORN PICKER, by Boris Artzybasheff. Media: *Liquitex, Polymer Tempera*, and designer's tube colors. (Courtesy: Avco Corporation and Benton and Bowles.)

Artzybasheff is known the world over for his humanized machines. His *Corn Picker* is a two-color illustration typical of these creations.

Whatman Cold Press Board was used as the support. A detailed drawing was made on separate paper and the whole design transferred to the board by tracing it over Carter's electric typewriter carbon paper with old-fashioned straight phonograph needles in a holder. (Artzybasheff has found that this type of carbon paper gives a sharp line which can be erased, if necessary, with lighter fluid on cotton swabs.)

After the design was established, all areas were given a golden undertone. This tone was achieved by mixing designer's Yellow Ocher and Umber colors with polyvinyl acetate emulsion. White highlights were established by mixing the emulsion with Winsor and Newton Permanent White. Glycerine was added to this white to smooth the paint, and to decrease the fast drying time. Washes of designer's Burnt Umber and *Liquitex* Mars Black followed.

The shadows on the picker machine are painted with Mars Black. The corn, in contrast, contains no black, so that the machine will stand out from its surroundings.

As he usually does, Artzybasheff gave this work a final spray of water-diluted *Liquitex* Medium for protection.

Figure 52. Illustration by Robert Weaver for "The Pitfalls of Personality Politics" by Thomas B. Morgan, 16×20 inches, 1961. Medium: *Liquitex*. (Reproduced by permission of Esquire Magazine © 1961 by Esquire, Inc.)

A wrinkled, weathered poster effect was obtained by Robert Weaver when he applied modeling paste to illustration board for this dual portrait of Nelson Rockefeller and Richard Nixon. (A split in the mock Rockefeller campaign poster reveals one of Nixon's underneath.) The modeling paste was troweled on with a palette knife before the design was begun. Weaver did not purposely strive to make the texture coincide with his subjects' features, although this occurred by happy accident in a number of spots. The edges of the "tear" were the only portions deliberately built up in form.

Black and white dominate the illustration; the only sections in color are the edges of the tear—the color there emphasizing the break between the two posters. (This is, of course, a symbolic as well as a painterly effect.) The portraits were drawn in directly over the paste texture and toned down with small watercolor brushes. Photographs of the two men were used as models.

Figure 53. Illustration by Bill Berry for "The Long Vigil." Media: *Liquitex* and charcoal. (Courtesy: *The Reporter* Magazine.)

This illustration was done for an article by Marya Mannes in *The Reporter* about the death and funeral of President John F. Kennedy. It shows the White House grounds in a winter setting. Although the original work was done in black and white, the magazine reproduction had an over-all light yellowish tint.

Linen cloth was soaked in water. When it was saturated, a Masonite panel was painted with a heavy coat of *Liquitex* Polymer Medium and the linen was placed over the Masonite and allowed to dry. Then another layer of medium was brushed over the linen. The medium acted both as a glue for the cloth and as a ground for subsequent work.

The basic black design was drawn on the linen with charcoal and fixed with a commercial spray. The synthetic emulsion colors were applied in a loose, dry-brush technique. Areas of the original cloth were allowed to show through as a darker tone. The light application of paint emphasized the texture of the linen, adding to the mood of the work.

Bill Berry has used *Liquitex* in many illustrations, as well as for fine art work. Often he incorporates sand or other additives with polymer medium or modeling paste for textural emphasis in his work.

tration. Even precise portraits are done with an emphasis on tonal values so that the features do not become overshadowed by fastidious color manipulations in reproduction. Color is used as a final wash or glaze technique only.

Weaver works on heavy illustration board. He first explores the subject and composition with many small sketches. Painting is direct and in some cases handled with speed and a sense of action if the subject invites such treatment—as it did in the two-page *Playboy* illustration (Color Plate 23, page 99). The paint is applied in a very modernistic, almost "action school," manner. The looseness and rapidity of execution help convey the story line immediately and forcefully. To meet a deadline, the work was mailed from New York to Chicago the same evening it was completed—a very risky procedure with any other medium.

C. C. Beall has developed a unique technique of painting with aqueous synthetics on glass and then removing the painting and applying it to another support. Beall perfected this film-transfer method of painting for several reasons. He is primarily a watercolorist and can employ thin watercolor techniques in painting on glass. Yet, when the work is transferred to another support such as canvas, the transparent paint takes on the quality of heavily painted oil. The technique may also produce an "aged" look. And it permits an unusual technique of painting in reverse perspective, which is described below.

Beall's film-transfer paintings begin by giving a sheet of glass a coat of acrylic emulsion white or white vinyl house paint. Scotch tape should be stripped around the edges of the glass before this priming so the film can be easily removed without producing ragged edges. The subject is painted over the white with polymer emulsion colors used in watercolor technique, with very thin washes. The finished work is allowed to dry for twenty-four hours. The pane of glass is then totally immersed in water and after a short soaking the Scotch tape is loosened. Carefully, the painting is peeled up from the glass. If portions are stubborn in removal, a little more time is given to

soaking. When the painting is free, the tape is cleanly cut away.

The whole process is based on the principle that the synthetic plastic emulsions will not stick to the smooth, shiny surface of glass and the films will detach themselves when water is applied over the glass. (When gloss medium is used the detachment is much easier.)

A support of Masonite or canvas or other material is then given a coat of polymer medium and the painting film is carefully pressed on so that wrinkles and air bubbles do not occur. Beall retouches portions after the film dries onto the support. The painting does not look like a watercolor but resembles heavy oil work.

Wrinkles and folds in the paint that occur in the transferring stage may be made on purpose, and Beall has become quite accomplished in producing paintings with a certain aged and weathered look. If Masonite is used as a support, he sometimes scores the wood with a mat knife before applying the paint film; this results in textural lines or restored-looking "cracks." Beall painted a portrait of General Grant on a private commission in a way that made the painting look as if it had been done by a comtemporary of the general.

Beall's reverse perspective method of painting is done on clear glass. He paints the foreground of the subject first with rather transparent colors and then completely covers this with background material. When the film is soaked off the glass, he attaches the *face* of the painting to the support. The final result is thus a mirror image of the painting as done on glass, with the foreground facing forward and the background receding in the distance. This technique can achieve a sense of great depth in a painting.

Beall says the plastic medium often produces effects more vivid and interesting than the artist could invent, and he sometimes incorporates these "accidents" into his precise commercial work. For example, when he sees interesting shapes or objects developing on his palette as the paints dry, he soaks and peels up the films and attaches them to supports as bases for later paintings. Beall also creates traditional watercolor and gouache paintings with poly-

mer emulsion colors. He is pleased with these synthetic-traditional techniques because if something goes wrong he need not throw away days of work, as he would if working in a traditional medium. He merely paints out the mistakes with white and proceeds with new watercolor washes over the offending portions.

Reproduction Techniques with Liquitex. Mr. Douglas Fales, a commercial artist of Montreal, has developed useful techniques using *Liquitex* products that reduce both time and expense in commercial reproduction. His work is with the popular Fluoro-Veloxes and similar methods of reproduction.

A coat of *Liquitex* Matte Medium seals the absorbency of paper and *Liquitex* Gesso kills the natural fluorescence found in some papers. Fluoro liquid mixed with either Matte or Polymer Medium in any proportion from 25 per cent to 50 per cent is quite versatile in producing gradations of grays and for textural effects in backgrounds. This leads to simplified steps in the reproduction of wash drawings due to sharper register by the fluorescent screen camera. A wash from gray into white requires no masking.

A paper or board coated with Matte Medium and Fluoro is no longer absorbent so the Fluoro washes do not sink in and lose their potency, actually being suspended as a sheet of fluorescent plastic on the surface. The engraver does not need to spray with a revivifying liquid to bring out the tonal contrasts. This allows the use of less expensive papers. If paper is extremely absorbent, a neutral and liberal wash of pure medium can be first laid on. When dry, the fluorescent-fluoro can be superimposed with grays.

Any error in making the Fluoro-Matte Medium-Black mixture for grays is easily corrected on the applied paint by using a swab of tissue or cotton wet with water. This means that the archaic retouch grays are no longer required.

Liquitex Gesso on bare paper not only prevents natural fluorescence of the paper, but also makes a perfect "drop-out" white when used on a *Liquitex* Fluoro ground or wash. Ink or pencil can be used on top of washes.

The surface texture of the paper is protected so erasures and rough handling are not apt to cause damage.

Acetate. Most of the polymer emulsions adhere very well to acetate and, therefore, can be used in color separation overlays. Acetate does not provide a durable surface for the polymers in fine arts use because the paints can be scratched off and will, at times, peel or "float up" when wet with water. They do work better than most other acetate colors, however.

Color Plate 22. PLANNER WILLIAM PEREIRA, by Boris Artzybasheff. Media: *Polymer Tempera, Liquitex,* powdered pigments, and tube colors. (*Time* Cover Portrait of William Pereira by Boris Artzybasheff; copyright Time Inc., 1963.)

Boris Artzybasheff has long created covers for *Time.* This painting of William Pereira appeared on the cover of the issue dated September 6, 1963.

The support was a sheet of hot-pressed Whatman board. A very detailed pencil drawing of the head was first made; then thin, very transparent watercolor washes established the facial tone. The watercolor was mixed with a small amount of polyvinyl acetate emulsion (*Polymer Tempera*) so that it would not dissolve when overpainted. Casein colors were combined with *Polymer Tempera* to build up features further. The head was finished with *Liquitex* colors and media ("They sink in less than any others," says Artzybasheff.) In this last procedure *Liquitex* was sometimes mixed with a dry pigment to give more tooth and body to the medium. Small red sable brushes were used throughout. The head was completed in approximately four days' working time.

The symbolic background was painted separately from the portrait. This whole area, as well as that for the sweater, was given a coat of *Liquitex* Mars Black—a ground Artzybasheff finds unusually responsive and which he often uses. Light areas were then painted out with his own combination of polyvinyl acetate emulsion and Winsor and Newton Permanent White. Painting continued with casein color and emulsion mixtures. The white squares are collage: paper cut out and glued with *Liquitex* Medium to the almost finished work. As a final step, a high-compression gun was used to spray *Liquitex* Medium diluted very thinly with distilled water over the whole painting.

Color Plate 23. Illustration by Robert Weaver for "On Her Majesty's Secret Service" by Ian Fleming, 20×30 inches, 1963. Medium: *Liquitex.* (Courtesy: *Playboy* Magazine. Art Director—Arthur Paul.)

Many pencil sketches and much research went into this illustration, but the actual painting itself was completed in a day's working time. The fast-moving action of the story was conveyed by loose, fast brush work and brilliant color native to the French locale. The support is heavy illustration board.

All but the portrait in the rear-view mirror at the top was directly painted. Colors were applied and overpainted for depth. Washes and glazes were also used. When a color was not correct, it was immediately rubbed off with a cloth. In the left portion of the work, the buildings originally extended to the side. Since this made the painting too "busy," the area was painted over with a translucent white glaze so that while the buildings would still show slightly, the work as a whole would be less cluttered.

The hood of the car was painted at the same time as was the upper portion of the work, and in the same brilliant colors. A black wash was brushed over the hood to produce the reflected effect. The direction of these strokes and the speed with which they were made also help give an impression of movement. The slight texture was created by the bubbles which form in a very water-diluted wash when it is vigorously brushed. Weaver often employs this bubble texture in his illustrations.

The face seen in the mirror—a portrait of an actor who has played the part of James Bond in the movies—was first painted in black and white, which freed the artist from color manipulations. Then color washes were quickly applied over the tonal areas. The effect is the same as if the whole work had been directly modeled in color. Weaver often uses this process in doing portraits.

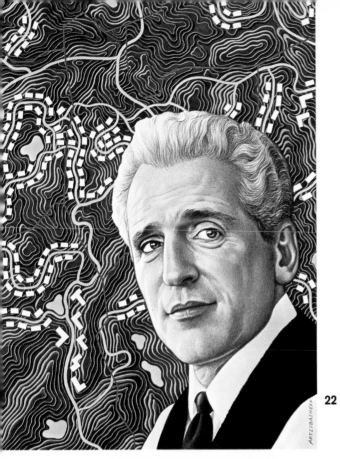

22

23

Chapter 13 / Acrylic Emulsion Brands: Liquitex, Politec, Aqua-Tec, Shiva

Liquitex.

Liquitex is an acrylic polymer emulsion produced by Permanent Pigments, Inc. It is an acrylic ester polymer in aqueous emulsion. The *Liquitex* line offers the most extensive list of colors and mediums available in the field since it is the only polymer produced in both jar colors and tube colors and the only line in which all of the accessory mediums discussed in the previous chapters can be found.

Colors. *Liquitex* colors come in two types: as a thick liquid in jars and with a body like oil color in tubes. Glass jars are of two-ounce, eight-ounce, pint and quart capacities. Gallons can be specially purchased. The tubes are of a two-ounce, metal, roll-up type. Pound-size tubes of white, black and *Liquitex* Gel Medium are also available. The two-ounce tube contains fifty per cent more paint then the standard studio-size tube.

There are thirty colors, including black and white, in each *Liquitex* line. The pigments available include complete chromatic ranges in both inherently opaque and inherently transparent colors. The more opaque colors as they come from the jar dry to a matte finish, the transparent colors have a slight gloss. Tube colors have a slight sheen. Many of the pigments are synthetic, such as Yellow Medium Azo, Napthol ITR Reds, Acra Red, Acra Violet and Dioxazine Purple.

Mediums. The *Liquitex* mediums are Polymer Medium (a gloss medium), Matte Medium, Gel Medium, and Matte Varnish. These come in jars. Gel Medium is available in both jars and tubes. *Liquitex* Gesso, Modeling Paste, and *Liquitex* Remover are produced in cans.

Freezing. *Liquitex*, like most other acrylic emulsions, is not affected by freezing. However, it is advisable not to flex or roll a painting in very cold weather because the paint surface becomes somewhat less pliable than usual.

Cost. The *Liquitex* colors cost from fifty cents to $1.25 in the two-ounce size. They are the lowest priced of the quality, pigmented polymer emulsions mentioned in this book.

Handling. *Liquitex* handles in the same manner as described in Chapters 1 through 12 of Part II. There are no exceptions or additions to what has been said. Because of this and because the majority of work illustrated in this book has been done with *Liquitex* it would be superfluous to discuss it further.

Politec

José Gutiérrez, a pioneer in synthetic painting for the past twenty years, formulated the acrylic polymer tempera which he calls *Politec* in 1954 and began producing it commercially in Mexico in 1957. He has written a book on the plastic media, *From Fresco to Plastics: New Materials for Easel and Mural Paintings*, published in Ottawa by the National Gallery of Canada, 1956 and 1959.

Politec is essentially the same type of paint as *Liquitex* jar colors and is worked in an identical manner. The company does not produce as wide a range of colors as does *Liquitex*. All of the *Politec* paints dry matte and are relatively opaque. *Politec* has a somewhat coarser pigment grind and is more viscous than *Liquitex*. It corresponds to *Aqua-Tec* (see below) in these qualities, but does not tend to separate in the jar as some of the *Aqua-Tec* colors presently do.

Two *Politec* varnishes are available, Barnis Sellador for medium gloss and Luzitron for a very high gloss. *Politec* manufactures no matte medium. Luzitron, which is not an emulsion but an acrylic resin varnish (a solution of acrylic resin in an organic solvent) may be used not only as a final varnish but also as a vehicle in which powdered pigments may be ground to form a resin paint.

The modeling paste used for *Politec* colors is called Plastelite—a mixture of polymer emulsion, marble dust, and celite. It has the consistency of very wet plaster and can be used for heavy impasto and modeling. When mixed with the paint it bleaches the colors slightly. An impasto of Plastelite one-eighth inch thick will dry overnight under normal weather conditions. Any heavier impasto should be built up with a number of thin coats, due to the danger of cracking. As with all emulsion pastes, medium should be added to prevent shrinkage cracking. (This has nothing to do with the inherent flexibility or durability but is only caused by too fast water evaporation.) When medium is added, the body of the paste is reduced and some of the water must evaporate before it returns to its original consistency.

Painters Using Politec. Arnold Belkin, a Canadian-born painter and muralist now working in Mexico, has been using *Politec* since 1956. In his early work with the medium he used the polymer emulsion for underpainting and accomplished the final overpainting with pigments ground in Luzitron varnish. In 1961 he was using the *Politec* colors for the entire painting and usually applying a final varnish of Luzitron.

The strength of polymer emulsion paint films was dramatically proven in the 1957 earthquake in Mexico City. Belkin had painted a mural in the Hilton Hotel in that city. The earthquake cracked the hotel in half, including the wall on which the mural was painted. That crack was the only damage suffered by the *Politec* mural; the paint film did not crack, peel, or chip as did the adjacent painted plaster.

Belkin in December, 1959, painted a mural on an exterior free-standing wall for a private home about a quarter of a mile from the Gulf of Mexico. Executed in *Politec* with a final varnish of several coats of Luzitron, this mural is still unaffected by weathering–even under climatic conditions which would cause ordinary house paint to fail after one or two years. I too painted an exper-

imental mural in *Politec* on an exterior cement wall of my Mexican home three years ago, covering parts of the mural with Luzitron. After nine months of weathering (including the Mexican rainy season of six months' duration), the varnished portions showed no change in color or brilliance. The unvarnished sections began to show color changes; colors mixed with white faded slightly. (Incidentally, friends in Mexico write me that the mural today, three years after completion, has developed no cracks or other visible signs of change.)

These two examples clearly suggest the use of acrylic resins, such as Luzitron, as a final varnish for all exterior murals painted with polymer emulsions. To insure against weathering effects for at least a five-year outdoor life, a coat of resin varnish should be applied every year or two.

I used *Politec* paints almost exclusively when I lived in Mexico during 1959 to 1961 and completed over two hundred paintings and studies in the medium. *Dance* (Figure 54) shows direct application of *Politec* without additives of any kind, on unprimed Masonite supports. The impastos seen in *Dance* are produced by the paint itself that was thickened slightly by allowing some of the water to evaporate before applying the paint. *On the Wharf* (Color Plate 24, page 105) also illustrates *Politec* used in slight impasto with thickened paint. The sketch called *Seated Man No. 5* (Figure 55) was done on a paper support.

Whither Goest Thou, Sixth to Ninth Hour (Color Plate 17, page 73) includes powdered fiber glass as a texturing material mixed with *Politec* paints. Many glazes and scumbles of color were used over this granular surface, as seen in the painting detail. Heavy impastos given by modeling paste contrast with flat unadorned areas.

Toby Joysmith's painting *Moonbirth* (Color Plate 25, page 105) illustrates a mixed media technique. The flat areas of underpainting were executed in many layers of thinly applied *Politec*. Ground pumice mixed with *Politec* provided the thick white impasto area. To obtain impasto line, black oil paint, given body by the addition of varnish, was squeezed from a fine-tipped plastic

sauce bottle. The painting was finished with glazes of oil colors which were allowed to partially dry and then were wiped. The layers of acrylic emulsion plus the thin oils result in a great depth and translucency. (The same effect may be accomplished with glazes of polymer emulsion paints. Color should be mixed with gloss medium until a slightly darker value and opacity than desired is obtained. The glaze is brushed on, or wiped on with a cloth. After a few seconds, use a soft, clean cloth to wipe the entire glazed areas. A very thin glaze results, and they can be built up in multiplicity.)

Joysmith has experimented with many synthetic media, alone and in combination, and at times uses very unorthodox methods of application. More of his technical innovations are discussed in Chapter 16.

Aqua-Tec

Aqua-Tec, produced by Bocour Artist Colors, New York, is a relatively recent addition to the field of synthetic emulsions formulated for the artist. It has thirty-three colors in its line as well as matte and gloss media, modeling paste, and gesso. Pure acrylic emulsion is its base, and therefore it has the same brilliance in color tone and the same versatility in handling as the other aqueous media previously examined. *Aqua-Tec* colors are of slightly thicker consistency, and handle more on the order of casein than tempera. They allow for oil-like manipulations with additives such as modeling paste and the inert clays. They are produced in two-ounce and larger jars, and in three-ounce wide mouth, plastic, squeeze bottles.

Some of the fine points of chemical formulation still need adjusting in the *Aqua-Tec* line at this writing. In some colors, the pigment tends to separate, leaving a layer of water and acrylic emulsion on top of a glutinous, sometimes stringy mass. Usually the paint can be stirred into a workable mixture. Leonard Bocour, president of the company, stated recently that such problems in color dispersion would shortly be solved.

Since *Aqua-Tec* is relatively new at this writing, very few examples of

←
Figure 54. DANCE, 48×36 inches, by Russell Woody, 1959–60. Medium: *Politec*.

Politec is somewhat coarser in texture and thicker in body than the other jar polymer emulsions. In this painting, the paint was used as it came from the jar. The heavy areas and the light impastos were the result of the medium's own qualities; no additives were incorporated.

The painting, on sanded Masonite, has a Yellow Ocher ground which shows through in several areas.

→
Figure 55. SEATED MAN NO. 5, 30×20 inches, by Russell Woody, 1960. Medium: *Politec*.

This is a sketch on paper—one of a series that preceded, and eventually led to, a finished painting. The paper was first brushed with clear water until it was thoroughly soaked. Form and design were then established on the wet paper with brushes fully loaded with *Politec* paints. The paint blurred into soft patterns and was allowed to dry for fifteen minutes. Painting then continued, and the hard lines and areas were established over the underpainting.

The work was from a model. The sketch took thirty minutes to complete, including the drying time between the two painting processes. A final varnish of *Politec* Medium was applied.

The paper was glued to a Masonite panel with *Politec* Medium and framed.

artists' work in the medium are available. Eugene Massin uses *Aqua-Tec* as an underpainting to which he applies oil overpainting in heavy impasto. (Figure 68 shows Massin's similar technique with Bocour's *Magna*.) Leo Manso often uses *Aqua-Tec* as a staining medium and in collage. *Tanka* (Figure 56) is a large collage, thirty-one by forty-one inches, saturated and stained with *Aqua-Tec* colors and medium. Torn muslin strips pigmented in this manner were glued to the Masonite support. Rice paper applied for textural emphasis was painted with *Aqua-Tec* gesso and opaque pigments. The backs of the paper and cloth strips were covered with polyvinyl glue and attached, sometimes one over the other, to the painting surface. Excess glue was removed with a damp cloth; the wetting did not remove any color because the polymer emulsions are waterproof after drying.

Shiva Acrylic Colors.

Shiva Acrylic Colors are the newest of the polymer emulsions to appear on the market. There are thirty-three colors in this line, which was intended to resemble oil paints. Some colors are of unusual hue, such as Permasol Yellow, Guignet's Green, and Green Gold. Colors are packaged in standard studio size, roll-up, metal tubes. *Shiva* Gloss Medium and *Shiva* Matte Medium are available in very wide mouth pint and quart jars. Liquid Gesso, Modeling Paste in pints and quarts, and Polymer Remover and Brush Cleaner in pints comprise the rest of the line.

The *Shiva* tube colors, although of an oil paste consistency when squeezed from the tube, tend to level and do not hold sharp brush or knife marks in most of the colors. To obtain a better viscosity the paints can be allowed to dry on the palette a short time before using. Since this method forms skins which have to be removed, the best way to "stiffen" the paint body is to add inert clays, which have already been discussed in relation to jar polymer emulsions.

I was able to test only one batch of *Shiva Acrylic* before this book went to the publisher. In these tests several colors on canvas and paper cracked when the support was rolled or when pressure was applied from the rear. The paints were inconsistent in viscosity and many had separation in the tube. They also contained numerous air bubbles which pit the paint surface. Problems of one kind or another have been found in almost every polymer emulsion produced when it first came on the market. The manufacturers, for the most part, soon find ways to correct the defects.

Color Plate 24. ON THE WHARF, 48×36 inches, by Russell Woody, 1960. Medium: *Politec*.

In this example of painting with *Politec*, an underpainting of Yellow Ocher and Burnt Siena was applied to a lightly sanded, untempered Masonite support with no ground. (Some of the underpainting still shows in the finished painting.) White areas were cut into this, and the whole was overpainted in the colors seen here. The *Politec* colors were allowed to thicken by the evaporation of water and were then handled with a palette knife and brush. The thick paints produced the impasto areas. No additives were used.

Color Plate 25. MOONBIRTH, 125×55 centimeters, by Toby Joysmith, 1959. Media: *Politec* and oil. (Collection: Dr. and Mrs. Robert Young, Mexico.)

In this mixed media painting, the blue base was built up of many layers of thinly painted *Politec*. The white of the moon was applied in thick plastic impasto, the paint being thickened with ground pumice stone, finely sifted through a cloth. The black was then "written in" with varnish-thickened oil paint squeezed from a plastic sauce bottle. The whole painting was glazed with umber, and the surface wiped clean when the glaze had partly dried. "The problem," explains artist Joysmith, "was to obtain a light blue which would at the same time appear luminous and in depth (i.e., so that you could look down through the layers of paint). The oil glaze was rubbed out in Perma-gel."

24

25

Figure 56. TANKA (THE TORCH), 41×31 inches, by Leo Manso, 1963. Medium: *Aqua-Tec* collage. (Courtesy: the artist.)

Tanka is a collage of bleached muslin saturated and stained with *Aqua-Tec* color and medium. Some rice paper, painted with *Aqua-Tec* Gesso and opaque *Aqua-Tec* pigment built into textures, was also used. The colored muslin was mounted in torn strips on a one-quarter-inch Masonite panel glued to a one-by-two-inch pine cradle for rigidity.

"This work evolved organically," explains artist Manso. "Layers of dry painted cloth were covered on one side with aqueous polyvinyl glue (Sobo, or Elmer's) and laid one over the other. For esthetic reasons, they were sometimes removed before setting. Each application was washed down with a fresh damp cloth to remove excess glue, but a slight film was left over the entire surface for protection.

"All the colored cloth and paper were absolutely dry before application; the wetting down did not in any way remove color from the surface."

Chapter 14 / Copolymer Emulsion Brands: *New Masters* and *Hyplar*

New Masters

New Masters colors are ready-to-use paints which have recently been introduced by *New Masters* Fine Arts Materials, a division of California Products Corporation, Cambridge, Massachusetts. They were developed with the specific intention of creating a synthetic paint that closely resembles oil paints in visual effect and in handling. *New Masters* is a copolymer—a combination of acrylic and polyvinyl polymers. The paints are highly viscous and look and feel like oil paints with a high surface sheen.

There are twenty-seven colors in the *New Masters* line including two types of black and Titanium White. The colors are packaged in translucent plastic tubes. These have the advantages of easy portability and non-breakability, but a disadvantage is that the artist will find it very hard to squeeze out all the paint. He must be precise in the amount of tube color squeezed onto the palette because the paints dry quickly and cannot be reused or dissolved in water upon drying. In cost, *New Masters* is comparable to first-line oil paints. The colors cover about the same area in brushing as comparable studio-size tubes of oil color. *New Masters* is the highest priced of the synthetic emulsions on the market. Two-ounce tubes range from seventy cents to two dollars. They are heavily pigmented, however, and make strong tints.

New Masters also offers a matte medium, a gloss medium, and a gesso. There is no modeling paste or gel in the line.

Painting with New Masters. *New Masters* paints handle in some ways like oils and in other ways like the other polymer emulsions. Like oils, they have a pull and a viscosity in brushing, and heavy impastos and textured paint may be applied directly without additions of any kind. But like the other polymer emulsions, water (not turpentine) is used as a thinner and for cleaning brushes. Supports, palettes, brushes, and grounds are the same as for other synthetic emulsions.

New Masters has an extended drying time in comparison with the fast drying jar emulsions and the slower drying tube colors in other lines. The paint without dilution by water or media takes three to four hours to dry. Glazes or thin washes dry in about thirty minutes; heavy impastos in five to ten hours. Paint films dry from the top down as water evaporates. If painting continues over a long period (six to eight hours or more), the paints become somewhat gummy and the partially set top skins become mixed with wet applications of color. To prevent this, direct *alla prima* painting should be discontinued after four hours. When the paint surface is dry to the touch, work can continue. If longer working times are desired, paints can be kept wet and manageable by periodic sprays with water from an atomizer. If too much water is used, the color will run.

New Masters paints may be thinned with water for watercolor or tempera techniques. This thinning with water reduces the drying time to about thirty minutes.

Pressure Adhesiveness. All the synthetic emulsions have some degree of pressure sensitivity; that is, when two surfaces of the media are placed face to face under prolonged or heavy pressure, they will stick together. They will also stick to other surfaces under pressure in hot weather. *New Masters* paints are especially high in pressure sensitivity. Therefore a canvas should not be rolled soon after painting, because the plastic will adhere to itself or to the back of the canvas (depending on which way the work is rolled). This acute pressure sensitivity disappears within six months, and *New Masters* paintings can then be handled in the same manner as other polymer emulsion works. Before this time, *New Masters* paintings should be stored vertically and there should be space between all of them. The "sticky" quality of the surface can be reduced by washing the paintings with mild soap and water once a week until the six month drying period has passed.

Hyplar

M. Grumbacher, Inc., produces the copolymer *Hyplar*. There are thirty-two colors packaged in jars of two-ounce, eight-ounce, pint, and quart size. Gloss Medium-Varnish, Matte-Medium-Varnish, Modeling Paste and Extender, Gesso, *Hyplar* Gel and *Hyplar* Remover complete the line.

Hyplar jar colors are thick in consistency, about the viscosity of a thin casein. Because *Hyplar* appeared on the market while this book was being written I have not had time to fully explore the paints and mediums. In a hurried examination I have found that a few of the colors crack when the canvas is pressed from behind. Some colors tend to separate from heavy watercolor paper when the paper is rolled or creased. Of course, paintings are not usually subjected to such extreme tests. However, most of the other polymer emulsions do not show these reactions.

Air bubbles in the paint caused a pock-marked surface in many of my tests. This effect is seen in many of the polymer emulsions when too vigorous brush work is done with water-thinned paints. Here it occurs with paints directly from the jar.

Hyplar colors hold brush strokes and knife marks better than any of the other jar type polymer emulsions with the exception of *Politec*. *Hyplar* Remover does not serve as a remover for other emulsion lines.

The reader is urged to make his own comparison tests with the various synthetic paints, and especially the newer ones. I can report only the more obvious advantages and disadvantages of a new product, since there has not been time to do exhaustive testing. Some of the defects in a new product are corrected soon after it appears on the market. Also, the reader may often find that my opinions differ from his.

Chapter 15 / Polyvinyl Acetate Emulsion: *Polymer Tempera*

Polymer Tempera was the first commercially produced synthetic emulsion medium offered the artist. In 1945, artist Alfred Duca initiated experiments with polyvinyl acetate ("PVA") to evaluate its usefulness as a fine arts medium. Polyvinyl acetate, being relatively new, was tried for many industrial purposes, from a highway pavement material to a filler between safety glass.

The basic problem in adapting PVA for fine arts purposes was to find a plasticizer which would make the somewhat brittle polymer. flexible without clouding the resulting plastic film, and also which would not migrate as plasticizers were prone to do. This was finally accomplished, and the resulting compound was patented and marketed under the name *Polymer Tempera* (a term that came to be known as nomenclature for all aqueous acrylic and synthetics; Duca simply adopted the generic term as an unregistered trade name).

Polymer Tempera is no longer sold as a ready-made material for painters and sculptors. Alfred Duca has released the formula to public domain, and he has graciously allowed the procedure for inclusion in this book.

General Characteristics. *Polymer Tempera* was developed as a universal fine arts medium, not only for the painter but for the sculptor and craftsman as well. Though *Polymer Tempera* is a vinyl-base emulsion, it has most of the characteristics of the acrylic and copolymer emulsions already discussed. The general characteristics of fine arts applications of the polymer emulsions, detailed in Part II, Chapters 1 through 12, are equally applicable to *Polymer Tempera*.

Polymer Tempera is an emulsion which is formulated by the artist. To make a paint, powdered pigments are added. The milky white medium, which dries transparent, has approximately the same body as *Politec*, *Aqua-Tec*, or *Liquitex* polymer mediums. It dries by the evaporation of water within ten to fifteen minutes when paint applications of normal thickness are used. Plastic particles suspended in the water fuse into one film, even in multiple applications, and are water insoluble upon drying.

Polymer Tempera has greater adhesive and binding properties than the acrylic emulsions and is recommended for procedures in which these properties are paramount. It is not as flexible as acrylic emulsions, however. Good plasticizers must be incorporated in a *Polymer Tempera* painting mixture (do not substitute for any of the materials listed in the formula below).

Unlike the acrylic emulsions listed in this book, *Polymer Tempera* coagulates and separates in cold temperatures, and is ruined if frozen. Canvases painted in *Polymer Tempera* should not be rolled in temperatures below 70 degrees Fahrenheit or cracking is likely to occur. Since most artists would use *Polymer Tempera* in a heated studio or home, its susceptibility to cold is not of great import.

Formula. The formula for producing five gallons of *Polymer Tempera* medium, as given by Alfred Duca, follows (manufacturers' names are given in parenthesis):

Five gallons Polyvinyl Acetate Emulsion (953-7 A) (Borden Chemical Division, Peabody, Mass., or any Borden plant office near you)

Sixteen ounces Resoflex R-296 (Cambridge Industries, Cambridge, Mass.)

Four ounces Cellosize (high viscosity WP-4400) dissolved in a small amount of water (Union Carbon and Carbide Co., New York, N.Y.)

One-eighth ounce Nacconal NRSF (National Aniline Division of Allied Chemical, Somerville, Mass., or Allied Chemical Corp., New York, N.Y.)

Procedure: To one gallon of Polyvinyl Acetate Emulsion slowly add the

Resoflex while stirring with a wood or glass implement. Let the mixture stand for twenty-four hours. Pour this into the remaining four gallons of PVA emulsion while stirring, and allow to stand twenty-four hours. Then add the Cellosize, pouring slowly while stirring so that troublesome agglomerates will not form. Finally, dissolve the Nacconal in a small amount of hot water, add to the other ingredients, and stir. (Never use water below 40 degrees Fahrenheit, to prevent coagulation.) The resulting medium should be stored in tightly capped jars.

The PVA emulsion is, of course, plastic resin polymerized in water. Resoflex is the only plasticizer which gives flexibility to the medium. Cellosize is a thickening agent which gives body and viscosity. Nacconal serves as a wetting agent which helps disperse the pigment when the latter is added to make a paint.

When raw materials are bought in quantity, the cost of one gallon of unpigmented *Polymer Tempera* comes to about $4.25. It is by far the least expensive of the polymer emulsion mediums of high quality.

Adding Pigments. To make a paint, powdered pigment is easily ground into the *Polymer Tempera* medium with a palette knife or other implement. Various quantities of pigment are required for various colors and the artist must experiment with each of his colors to determine the quantities. Generally, if he rubs up enough pigment to make a soft paste, he is more or less safe.

Many pigment colors are not chemically compatible with the synthetic resins (either acrylic or vinyl), and some others require an abnormal amount of wetting, dispersing, grinding, or plasticizing. Such pigments are not suitable for the artist to use to make his own paints. A fairly safe and tested palette includes the following pigments (which must be of a good grade):

Titanium Oxide White
Venetian Red
Red iron oxides
Cadmium reds
Cobalt Blue
Ultramarine Blue
Ultramarine Violet
Cerulean Blue
Cadmium oranges
Cadmium yellows
Yellow ochres
Burnt and Raw Umber
Burnt and Raw Siena
Chrome Oxide Green
Iron Oxide Black (Mars Black)

For best results, paints should be ground immediately for each painting session. Mixtures of *Polymer Tempera* and pigment ideally should not be stored for extended periods. If high quality pigments are used, the paints can be stored for short periods in glass or plastic jars with tight lids. Metal containers may discolor the medium because it reacts chemically with iron, tin, and galvanized metals.

For more convenient handling, many artists grind pigment into water and store the solution in tightly sealed jars until ready to use the color. This system also assures consistent color better than grinding each day's paint from scratch. To form a paint from such water ground pigments, they are mixed in a ratio approximating one part color to two parts PVA emulsion, some colors taking more, some less.

The artist who grinds his own paints will not achieve the same consistency in each color, such as the manufacturers achieve. One pigment may produce a relatively long and stringy paint, and another may be as fine and soft as warm butter. Some artists, myself included, prefer such peculiarities among pigments, while others have become so accustomed to the smooth and constant mixtures achieved by mass production that they would be uncomfortable with the idiosyncrasies.

Gloss and Matte. *Polymer Tempera* paints produce a medium gloss. A semigloss surface can be obtained by making a wax emulsion mixed four to one: four parts medium to one part beeswax. This mixture is heated in a double boiler and painted over the work while warm. If a higher gloss is desired, the encaustic-type varnish can be polished with a soft cloth to increase its luster. For a matte surface, Celite or calcium carbonate is added to this wax medium.

Gesso Ground. *Polymer Tempera* can be used on any type of support except those with smooth and shiny surfaces.

If it is desirable, a gesso ground can be used to create a reflective painting surface and one which has a fine tooth. I have used the following PVA emulsion gesso for priming supports.

Ingredients (by volume, not weight) for about two quarts of gesso:
½ pint *Polymer Tempera* medium
1 ounce Resoflex R-296 (optional and in addition to the Resoflex included in the PVA)
1 quart water (distilled or fairly mineral-free)
1 pint Titanium White
½ pint Paris White (native calcium carbonate—general name is "whiting")

Procedure: Slowly pour Resoflex into medium while stirring. (I use Resoflex, a pasticizer, to prevent cracking when excess additives are used, such as marble dust or more white. More *Polymer Tempera* medium may be added instead of using the Resoflex.) Add water and mix gently but thoroughly. Combine the dry ingredients and sift slowly into the liquid mixture. Be sure that all pigment has been wet completely and stirred in before adding more. Strain through a fine wire screen. Make a scratch test to determine the strength of the gesso. If any white color flakes off or can be wiped off with a damp cloth, add more PVA medium. To do this, dilute with a combination of one part *Polymer Tempera* to three parts water. More tooth can be achieved by adding to the mixture fine marble dust which has been saturated with medium.

Alfred Duca. Alfred Duca has painted with *Polymer Tempera* since he invented it in 1945, and other artists have used the medium for almost as long with excellent results. Among these are James Brooks, Karl Zerbe, Syd Solomon, Hyman Bloom, and Boris Artzybasheff. (See Chapter 12 for Artzybasheff's use of *Polymer Tempera*.)

Duca's work exploits the brilliance and luminosity of the medium. He uses many glazes one over the other with a high gloss finish. To heighten the gloss even more at times, each of these successive coats is quickly wiped with denatured alcohol. This is a risky procedure if the film is low in polymer content in that the alcohol may disturb

Figure 57. TERN WINGS, about 16×54 inches, by Alfred L. Melenbacker, 1962. Media: PVA emulsion, cement, wood flour. (Collection: Dr. and Mrs. Wells Goodrich.)

The support of this PVA-emulsion hanging relief sculpture is plywood. Holes were drilled in the plywood so that copper wire could be inserted from the front and fastened to the back. The front ends of the wires were then covered with copper screening and generally shaped into the wing forms that were to be the key to the over-all design.

A one-half-inch application of polymer cement (see caption for Figure 58) and redwood sawdust was troweled onto the support, and the background was shaped.

When the base had dried, polymer cement mixed with white sawdust was applied to the screen-and-wire forms and built in successive coats to the desired relief. (Before each layer was added, the dry mass was soaked with water so that it would not absorb medium and water from the wet cement and thus reduce the latter's adhesive qualities.) The wing areas were further modeled by carving, sawing (with a hack saw), filing, and sanding. Finally, coats of PVA emulsion were given the piece for weather resistance before it was placed outdoors.

In the completed piece, the redwood flour provides notable color and textural contrast with the white wood flour.

underlying paint films and must be done as fast and as exactly as possible.

As a Medium for Sculpture. Like most of the synthetic emulsions that have been discussed earlier, *Polymer Tempera* is well suited for three-dimensional and sculptural techniques. A very strong binder, it will not only cement aggregates but will actually give more cohesion than most of the other synthetics.

Small pieces made with PVA emulsion mixed with papier-mâché or powdered plastic materials can be modeled like clay, carved when partially set, and sanded, chiseled, or ground when dry. For large sculpture pieces, including outdoor work, the low initial investment in the medium (due, of course, to the artist's making it himself) keeps final costs to a minimum.

When the sculpture is to be of substantial size, the PVA emulsion should be mixed with cement or plaster, sand, and aggregates. The medium is added in proportion to the amount of cement or plaster used, and should not exceed twenty-five per cent of the dry mix. Water is added to make a workable mixture. If a type of concrete is desired, the cement, PVA emulsion, and water are first combined, the amount of water used depending on the cement mixture and the absorbency of any aggregates; then the quantity of sand and/or aggregates suggested in the manufacturer's directions is added. Enough cement and medium must be used to surround and bind the aggregates; too little results in a mass that will crumble and crack on exposure to weathering. Rock, cracked and powdered marble, pottery pieces, glass, wood pulp, shredded asbestos or fiber glass, ground cork, powdered plastics, etc., may be incorporated as textural admixtures.

If direct modeling is intended, the sculptural medium should be stiff. Soft material, such as sawdust, shredded paper, flour, or vermiculite will help cohesion if mixtures do not hold together well. When the piece dries, additions can be made at any time if the surface is wetted with water-thinned emulsion before application.

A large cardboard form can be constructed in the general shape of the sculpture piece, using corrugated cardboard held together with strips of cloth soaked in PVA emulsion. The sculpture mixture is then poured into the form and then allowed to harden. When a soft set is achieved, the cardboard is removed, and the sculpture can be carved with a knife. After it reaches full hardness, it can be chiseled or polished.

For colored sculpture, powdered pigments can be added in the initial mixing procedure. It's possible, of course, to paint over sculptural work, but the color is more permanent when it is incorporated in the basic materials.

To give *Polymer Tempera* sculpture greater resistance to weathering, it can be coated with *Lucite* (see Part III, Chapter 1) dissolved in one of the volatile thinners. But any artist who so coats his work should beware of toxicity and be sure to have adequate ventilation.

PVA emulsion sculpture should not be dried too quickly. A slow cure results in greater strength. If drying has to be done in dry or hot weather, the work should be covered with a damp cloth to reduce rapid and excessive loss of moisture; large masses should be allowed to set for five or more days in this manner.

Alfred L. Melenbacker of Wellfleet, Massachusetts, has employed the PVA emulsion medium for pouring table tops and lamp bases as well as the sculpture and high bas-relief reproduced here. His high relief, *Tern Wings* (Figure 57),

111

is built on a copper-wire-and-screen armature. It has gone through a hurricane and severe storms without any signs of cracking or other weakness.

Melenbacker's sculptures in the round, *Old Stallion* and *Greater Yellow Legs* (Figures 58 and 59), were built on copper-and-brass armatures in multiple applications of polymer cement. Expanded mica was added in the mixing process to keep the pieces light.

These are only a few instances of how *Polymer Tempera* can be employed in sculptural techniques. Others are given in Part II, Chapter 11, and the artist will undoubtedly find many more ways of using the polymer emulsions which suit his own methods and intent of expression.

Other Polyvinyl Acetate Emulsions. There are several small manufacturers

of PVA emulsions, especially on the West Coast. They produce pigmented vinyl emulsions in jars and plastic squeeze bottles.

Their main advantage is that the low quality permits them to be sold at very reduced prices. They should not be used for serious fine arts work. A better and less expensive paint can be achieved by grinding pigments into industrial polymer emulsions (see next chapter).

Figure 58. OLD STALLION, ca. 15 inches high, by Alfred Melenbacker, 1962. Media: PVA emulsion, cement, expanded mica. (Courtesy: D. E. Kendall Art Gallery, Wellfleet, Massachusetts.)

Figure 59. GREATER YELLOW LEGS, ca. 10 inches high, by Alfred H. Melenbacker, 1963. Media: PVA emulsion, cement, expanded mica. (Courtesy: D. E. Kendall Art Gallery, Wellfleet, Massachusetts.)

The medium for this sculpture is generally termed *polymer cement*. It is a mixture of four parts Portland cement, one part polyvinyl acetate emulsion, and enough water to make the combination workable. *Old Stallion* was built on a copper pipe armature, embedded in a pre-cast polymer cement base. Expanded mica was added to the PVA mixture for bulk and lighter weight. It was modeled in successive layers (none over one-half inch in thickness), each layer being allowed to dry before another was applied. After the initial hand-shaping, the dried work was carved and sanded to its final shape and sheen.

Like *Old Stallion* (Figure 58), *Greater Yellow Legs* was made with polymer cement. It was built on free-standing brass rods which were fastened temporarily to a work-board during construction. The body forms were fashioned with copper wire and copper screen armatures; polymer cement was applied over these. Copper and brass are often used for such purposes with the PVA emulsion, because the emulsion reacts with various other metals.

The brass rods were sunk into a brick block which was attached as a permanent base.

Chapter 16 / Industrial Polymer Emulsion

There are a number of industrial plastic emulsions, both acrylic and vinyl, which the artist may use as the base for pigmenting his own paints, if he so desires. These clear emulsions often serve very well as a paint medium—as long as the artist knows which emulsions are suitable for fine arts work and follows the instructions given by manufacturers for making paints. Substandard formulations will not achieve satisfactory handling qualities or adequate paint films.

Excellent grades of acrylic emulsion, called Rhoplex AC 33 and Rhoplex AC 34, can be obtained from Rohm and Haas Company. Booklets are available describing the composition of Rhoplex and how it may be combined with pigments for both interior and exterior use. It can also be used in sculpture. There are several other acrylic and vinyl emulsions available which the artist may investigate on his own with the help of the manufacturers. I consider Rhoplex the most reliable.

Toby Joysmith, a British artist now working in Mexico, often grinds his own pigments into an acrylic sealer. (He also employs *Politec*—see Chapter 13—and *Eterna*, produced locally by Casa del Arte, Mexico City.) Joysmith has a background which enables him to determine which of the industrial synthetics suit his purpose. He has used

synthetics in his own painting for a number of years and has taught the use of synthetics at the University of the Americas in Mexico City.

Joysmith uses Masonite as a support and gives it a heavy coat of the acrylic sealer; he paints on either the smooth or the rough side of Masonite, depending on the adhesive qualities he needs. He applies at least four coats of acrylic emulsion white as a ground, and, if he decides to paint on the rough side, he adds sifted, powdered pumice stone to the last two coats.

Joysmith describes his technique as follows: "I tend to draw with a point into a wet medium mixture which is spread on the support. At times I have used wool yarn dipped in the emulsion to create these structure lines. Forms are defined with a spatula or painting knife. The mixtures I use to obtain textures vary in composition but are made basically with Resistol 850 (an industrial polymer glue), plaster, powdered pumice stone, and water. If I want a rougher texture I add sawdust or even powdered cork. For very fine textures I sift pumice through a cloth. The textures are built up with a knife or the fingers, or else a flat board is dragged across the surface.

"If the painting begins to go wrong I attack it with a stone chisel and hammer and obliterate most of the texture. This

generally gives a good base for future operations.

"When the mixture is dry (in about two or three hours, depending on its thickness), I begin to adjust the values in each form by using scumbles or glazes—generally both. I use many glazes, building hot on cold, and never allow any dead color to stand which has not been modified by a glaze. My glazes are plastic ones, made with acrylic emulsion medium (*diluyante* in Mexico), pigment, and water. The painting is always flat on a table and I use many white and off-white glazes in preference to the more traditional colors."

Four of Joysmith's highly textural, metamorphic paintings are illustrated here: *Lawrence of Arabia*, *Landscape with Pyramid*, and two of the five panels that constitute his mural *Motherhood* (Color Plate 26, page 120, and Figures 60 and 61).

Another artist who grinds his own pigments is young New Yorker Mario Yrisarry. His emulsion is the polyvinyl acetate emulsion Darex Everflex G, produced by the Dewey and Almy Chemical Division of the W. R. Grace and Company. Yrisarry came to the synthetics out of necessity. Oils and turpentine used to dissolve portions of the rubber stamps which are essential to his technique and cause very sticky

Figure 60. LANDSCAPE WITH PYRAMID, 60×80 centimeters, by Toby Joysmith, 1961. Medium: Acrylic emulsion. (Collection: René Anselmo, Mexico City.)

Toby Joysmith prepared his Masonite panel for this painting with several coats of commercial acrylic emulsion. The basic pyramid structure was constructed of balsa wood (the type used for building model airplanes), and the textural areas were outlined with wool yarn to produce raised, free-form lines. Both materials were attached with medium. The rough and crusty surface resulted from a mixture of Resistol 850, plaster, powdered pumice stone, and water. It was built up with the fingers and a palette knife. A flat board was dragged across the wet mass to flatten certain portions. Dry, the roughened surfaces were the original brown-gray of the mixture (not too much plaster had been mixed in). The entire painting was then covered with white and off-white glazes. Finally, accents were painted on matte and later glazed.

Grayed and ocher earth colors predominate in the painting with accents of black and orange.

Figure 61, I and II. BIRTH and MOTHER AND CHILD (two parts of the five-panel mural MOTHERHOOD), each panel 1 meter, 60 centimeters × 2 meters, by Toby Joysmith, 1962. Medium: Acrylic emulsion. (Courtesy: the artist.)

These are two panels of a mural commissioned by the Women's Hospital in Mexico City. There are five panels in the series, done on acrylic-sealed Masonite. Four of the panels—*Inpregnation, Gestation, Birth* (I), and *Mother and Child* (II)—are two meters wide. The fifth, a vertical panel, is two meters high. It represents the family trinity: Father, Mother, Child.

Both these reproductions illustrate the many textural additives and the variety of surface quality that are typical of much of Joysmith's work. Balsa wood strips, pumice stone, sawdust, plaster, and wool yarn formed the bases of various areas. These materials were either mixed with plastic emulsion (this was true of the plaster, sawdust, and pumice) or attached with the vehicle (as were the balsa and yarn). Lines were incised (see upper left portion of *Mother and Child*), built with additives, and modeled with a knife or the fingers (see the pyramid steps, portions of the figures, and adjacent areas).

The predominant colors are earth pigments with sharp accents of greenish blue and orange. The panels were painted flat, on top of a large table.

115

and gummy masses. A chemist friend suggested an emulsion as the answer.

Yrisarry's large-scale paintings are a combination of printing, stenciling, spraying, and brush work. He makes hundreds of sketch designs before proceeding with the painting proper. When he has decided on a composition, he tacks a large canvas on a blank wall and paints it with an overall solid color. Then he cuts rubber-mat runners (the kind usually associated with halls or steps) to shape, coats them with his mixed color, and presses them against the canvas. He prints the same pattern over itself many times in various colors, so that different hues, shades, and tones show through one another.

At times Yrisarry combines or contrasts these printed surfaces with very fine, soft sprayed areas, using his pigmented polymer medium in a compressed air gun. He also affixes stenciled shapes to his canvas and sprays over them. This results in a hard edge that dissolves into soft colors, so that the viewer can hardly tell where the shapes end and the background begins.

Yrisarry's painting is very direct. He mixes powdered pigment with Everflex and applies colors to the canvas, in one manner or another, without using any additives of any kind. Examples of his work are his *Untitled* painting No. 1, a detail from his *Untitled* painting No. 2 and a detail from the painting studies that cover the walls of his studio (Figures 62, 63, and 64).

Some artists use pigmented commercial house paints (with either a vinyl or an acrylic base) at times to augment fine art emulsions. They are not recommended for serious work, however. The ingredients and pigments of such house paints are of questionable quality. They should only be used for underpainting, and only if the plastic base is known to be reliable in durability and adhesion.

Figure 62. UNTITLED painting 2, 72×84 inches, by Mario Yrisarry, 1963. Medium: *Darex Everflex G* (PVA polymer emulsion). (Courtesy: the artist.)

Mario Yrisarry had to turn to aqueous synthetic media as a necessity when he began to use pieces cut from molded rubber hall mats to print shapes on his canvases. He found that the solvents in most paints dissolved his printing surfaces. A polymer emulsion, *Darex Everflex G* (produced by W. R. Grace and Co.) served his purpose, however, so he started to grind powdered pigments (purchased from Fezandie and Sperrle, Inc., New York City) into the vinyl plastic vehicle.

In this particular painting the commercially primed canvas was given an over-all brushing of solid color. Some of this ground color shows through the printed shapes. The multiple prints were applied in small sections. Then adjacent masses were blocked in over the solid ground. Each print took from twenty to twenty-five minutes to dry before work could proceed.

The stars seen in the upper portion are part of the original pattern of the molded hall runner, as are the side slits. These rigid, machine-made patterns are contrasted with the organic structure which Yrisarry builds from them.

Figure 63. UNTITLED Painting 2 (detail), 12×12 inches, by
Mario Yrisarry, 1963. Medium: *Darex Everflex G* (PVA polymer
emulsion). (Courtesy: the artist.)

This is a detail of one of the shapes Yrisarry makes by stamping
sections of rubber mats on canvas. Here the same shape has
been printed over itself several times. The frosty configurations
result from heavy paint piled on the rubber surface, placed
against the canvas, and pulled away before the paint sets.

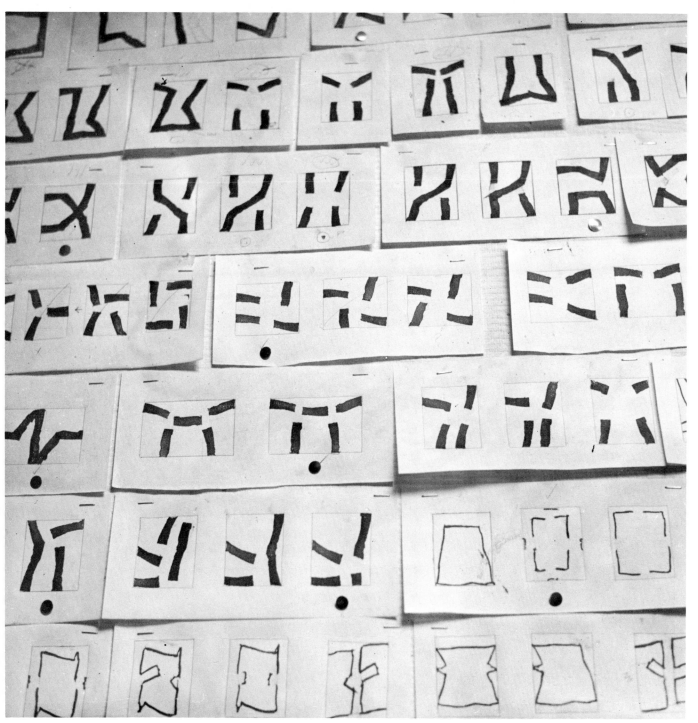

Figure 64. Detail of painting studies, by Mario Yrisarry. (Courtesy: the artist.)

This photo shows a small segment of a wall in Yrisarry's studio which is covered with hundreds of quick studies. "Only one or two of these will ever become the basis for a painting," says the artist. They are used mostly to explore the compositional developments which may apply to his printed, stenciled work.

Color Plate 26. LAWRENCE OF ARABIA, 96×130 centimeters, by Toby Joysmith, ca. 1961. Medium: Acrylic emulsion. (Collection: The Honourable Julian Byng, London.)

This heavily textured acrylic emulsion painting was done on Masonite which had been given a ground of the emulsion. While the artist always uses Masonite as a support in any case, it would not have been advisable to build such thick areas on a more flexible surface (e.g., canvas), because the overload of additives would have lowered the pliability of the vehicle too greatly. It's not that the longevity of the material on canvas would have been affected, but rolling, bending, or accidental blows might well have caused cracks.

Joysmith built up the linear textures with string and wool yarns soaked in the emulsion, which served as a glue. Massive areas were accomplished with mixtures of medium and powdered pumice. Forms were defined with a palette knife. The whole work was then painted with powdered pumice stone, finely sifted and mixed with clear emulsion. The finished, sandy surface was heavily glazed with white to which a little blue had been added. A chisel was used to "excavate" the strong blue and black area in the acrylic mass, and final paint was applied.

The emulsion used was a commercial type sold in Mexico. Powdered pigment was ground into this.

PART III
OTHER SYNTHETIC MEDIA

Chapter 1 / Acrylic Resin Solutions

Part II of this book has concerned synthetic resins that are *suspended* in a water medium. These are emulsions, not solutions. In an emulsion the resin is present as microscopically fine plastic particles; in a solution one material is *dissolved* in another so that a clear, homogeneous mixture results—as when sugar is dissolved in water, or, in the artist's experience, as when damar is dissolved in turpentine to form a varnish.

The two classes of synthetic resins (acrylics and vinyls) which are suspended in water to form the emulsions can also be dissolved in appropriate solvents to form plastic varnishes which are used as painting media. The kind of acrylic resin used for these solutions is quite similar to the kind of acrylic resin used in emulsions. The vinyl resins, however, are somewhat different, being usually the vinyl chloride acetate "copolymer" for solution-varnishes rather than the polyvinyl acetate or the acrylic-polyvinyl copolymer discussed for use in the emulsions.

There is only one commercially available line of artist's colors using a resin solution: *Magna* colors, manufactured by Bocour Artist's Colors, Inc., which use an acrylic medium. Other than this the artist must make his own resin paints by grinding powdered pigments into the resin solution.

Solvents and Toxicity. Water cannot be used with synthetic resin solutions or varnishes. Organic solvents are necessary both to make the initial solutions and to thin the paints made from them. Many of these solvents, such as acetone, toluene and xylene, have an appreciable degree of toxicity. Turpentine, which is less toxic, can be used with a few. Some persons are rather sensitive to the effects of the stronger solvents, and it is essential that one be careful to maintain very adequate ventilation or the solvents can become a dangerous health hazard. Also, all these organic solvents are flammable.

The resins themselves are innocuous in the state in which they are used, are stable and chemically inert, and are not known to produce any allergic reactions.

Making Solution Paints. Making one's own colors in synthetic resin solutions is frequently done by artists, although it is not an easy task. For one thing, the fast evaporating solvent makes handling difficult. Other problems are that pigments do not break up readily in such solutions, they require longer grinding, and they show roughness more frequently in the finished paint because of the lower binder content one has to work with in the solutions. Then there is the ever present problem of knowing what the limit is for each pig-

ment relative to the quantity of medium to produce a permanently flexible paint. Experience with the type of resin used, the solvent, and the type and quality of pigment selected is the only answer.

Why Use Resin Paints? In the face of difficulties mentioned above it must be explained why some artists use the resin paints as opposed to the polymer emulsions. Probably the most often quoted reason is the fast drying time. Many of the resin paints, due to the fast drying volatile thinners or solvents used, dry within five minutes. They are the most durable paints produced. Because the plastic films that form are even more tightly bound than the polymer emulsion films, they can withstand weathering better, and are, therefore, a better paint to use outdoors. This is not to say that resin paints will not show deterioration after a few years outdoors. But they are the most permanent we have today.

Some acrylic resin paints can be mixed with oils and turpentine to form a faster drying, more durable, oil paint. Painters who want oil-like handling and characteristics sometimes use the synthetic resins with oils to achieve this end (although typical oil paint characteristics can be obtained with the tubed polymer emulsions). The disadvantages of mixing resin solutions with oils are listed below in relation to the particular resins used.

Perhaps the main reason that artists use the resin paints is a very unsatisfactory one: artists, by word-of-mouth, became acquainted with the resin solutions before learning of the other synthetics.

How to Use Acrylic Resin Paints. Acrylic resins must be bought in their dry state (with a few exceptions where the manufacturer supplies an already dissolved acrylic) and dissolved in organic solvents to make a resin solution medium. Water is not used for any purpose, either for thinning or cleaning, as the resin solutions will not mix with water. Paints are made by grinding dry pigments into the clear resin solutions. The paints are thinned with the same organic solvent used to make the resin solution, and cleaning of brushes, palette, etc., is done with the same solvent. Dried paint can be used again when dissolved with the solvent; therefore, there is no loss of dry paints on the palette.

Painting with resin solutions must be done quickly and with decision because the paints dry very fast and because the solvents in the paint will pick up or muddy and dissolve underlying paint if worked too long or hard over a specific area. This difficulty does not arise, however, with those resins which are dissolved in turpentine, except to the degree experienced in oil painting.

Any type of support may be used with pure resin solutions: canvas, Masonite, paper, cement block, even metal and glass. Painting is direct, with no priming required, although for very rough supports such as cement a coat of clear resin solution (unpigmented) will facilitate later brush work. Because of the acrylic's qualities of excellent adhesion and flexibility, any amount of impasto can be applied without danger to the durability of the painting.

Durability. The resin solutions dry by the evaporation of the solvent, which leaves a very tightly knit plastic film. The films are much less porous than those formed with polymer emulsions (which dry by the evaporation of water causing the suspended plastic particles to coalesce and leave microscopic spaces between some of the particles). Therefore, unpigmented solutions of acrylic resin form excellent final protective varnishes and can be used as such over all works done with the synthetic media, including the emulsions. The films resist all normal weathering including ultraviolet rays, as well as most chemical fumes, acids, and alkalines. They do not yellow with age, and durability by present tests is exceptional.

Lucite. Several acrylic resins are produced today which are suitable for making paints for fine arts purposes. The brands with which I am most familiar are *Lucite* and *Acryloid*. Therefore, these receive attention here, though acrylics under other trade names may be reasonably assumed to have similar properties and methods of handling.

Lucite, a product of E. I. DuPont de Nemours and Company, was one of the earliest acrylic resins produced in this country. It has been used for a great variety of industrial purposes, from clothing fabrics to automobile finishes, since the 1930's.

Three types of *Lucite* can be used for formulating artists' paints: *Lucite* 44, a butyl methacrylate polymer; *Lucite* 45, an isobutyl methacrylate polymer; and the copolymer *Lucite* 46, a 50/50 n-butyl/isobutyl methacrylate. The methacrylate polymers used in all three produce hard and tough films but have low flexibility; the butyl esters, also present in all three, have good flexibility, and thus the combination of the two produces the desired characteristics for a paint film.

To form a solution or varnish which can be used as a basis for a paint, *Lucite* is bought in its dry crystal form and dissolved in toluene, xylene, or turpentime. *Lucite* 44 is compatible with turpentine; the other types should be used with the stronger solvents.

The quantity of thinner used depends on the paint consistency desired; a common proportion is three parts solvent by weight to two parts resin. The *Lucite* 44-turpentine medium gives a matte result, and the turpentine slows down the drying time of the *Lucite*. Toluene and xylene as solvents provide a faster drying time and a more glossy finish.

To make a paint, powdered pigments are mixed with the *Lucite* varnish. Some traditional pigments will not mix satisfactorily with either the acrylic or vinyl solutions; thus the palette of synthetic resin paints is somewhat restricted. A safe list of pigments is given in Chapter 15, page 110. If mixed correctly, the paints have excellent cohesive qualities, retain the brush stroke very well, are very fast drying and very flexible.

Lucite is obtained from Du Pont distributors, who will usually ship the required amount direct to the artist (although some sources require a large minimum order). Thinners can be purchased at any large paint store.

The unpigmented *Lucite* varnish, incidentally, can be used as a priming for oils. It protects the canvas from attack by the oil medium. Underpainting with *Lucite* paints is also possible for oil paintings.

Oil with Lucite. *Lucite* has a certain tolerance to oil, and the synthetic resin can be mixed with oil in two ways: by adding linseed oil and turpentine to the pigmented acrylic medium, or by adding actual oil paints from the tube to the pigmented medium. A semigloss surface results with the addition of oils.

The mixing of oils or resin oil media with *Lucite* is not highly recommended, however. DuPont states that *Lucite* is incompatible with such resins as damar and copal which are often found in painting media. And *Lucite* is partially insoluble in linseed oil. Also, oils oxidize and acrylics do not; this produces two different types of film-forming action, which, in theory at least, should be avoided. Many artists, including James Brooks, Karl Zerbe, Arnold Belkin, and Syd Solomon, formerly used *Lucite* and oil in paintings but have switched to the polymer emulsions.

Oil and *Lucite* have been combined successfully, however. Painter Gabor Peterdi often uses a mixture of equal parts of *Lucite*, linseed oil, and turpentine. He prefers *Lucite* 44 because it is much more flexible than *Lucite* 45. Before he adopted *Lucite*, Peterdi used damar varnish. In comparison, Peterdi found that damar was more brittle and cracked more easily than *Lucite*, that the synthetic was never as glossy as damar, and that *Lucite* seemed to produce more luminosity. In addition, the fast drying time common to all the synthetic resins made *Lucite* preferable.

Adolph Gottlieb has developed a paint mixture that gives him just the quality he wants, coupling extreme thinness with opacity of color. He dissolves *Lucite* 44 crystals in a half and half mixture of toluene and xylene and then adds oil colors to this vehicle. This medium gives a liquid flow and viscosity that Gottlieb has been unable to duplicate in any other manner. It permits paint to be literally flipped into configurations with the palette knife, as in *Petaloid No. 2* (Figure 65). Gottlieb's work has an immediacy of expression and an economy of means that are aided by such a fast drying medium as his *Lucite* mixture provides. He also uses *Lucite* 45, *Lucite* 46, *Rhoplex AC 33*, and *Magna*. The *Rhoplex* does not produce as opaque a paint as he prefers nor does it have the viscosity, while *Magna* picks up on overpainting too much for his liking. Gottlieb usually grounds his paintings with such commercial aqueous emulsion synthetics as *Dutch Boy* Latex White over large, stretched canvas.

Acryloid. *Acryloid* acrylic ester resins are manufactured by Rohm and Haas Company. Several *Acryloid* varieties are suitable for fine arts. *Acryloid* B-44 is noted for exceptional adhesion. *Acryloid* B-72 and B-82 are comparable varieties; B-82 is available at lower cost. José Gutiérrez has used the B-72 and B-82 resins to great advantage. His method of preparing these resins is as follows: "Weigh 600 grams of toluene in a container, add 400 grams of resin B-72 or B-82, *slowly*, a few grains at a time in a rapid laboratory mixer. When every grain is completely dissolved it is ready to use. *Keep in a tightly closed container.*" (José Gutiérrez. *From Fresco to Plastics.* Ottawa: The National Gallery of Canada, 1956, 1959.)

A slower but equally effective method is to pour the toluene or a half and half mixture of toluene and xylene into a glass container with the resin crystals. The *Acryloid* will dissolve in about the same time it takes damar crystals to form a varnish—roughly from one to five days, depending on the consistency desired. The process of straining out impurities associated with the making of damar varnish is eliminated, since the synthetic resins are usually very pure.

Rohm and Haas also offers a soft acrylic that comes in 40 per cent solution in mineral spirits. This is called *Acryloid* F-10. One can simply add turpentine to this ready-made solution to bring the concentration down to close to 30 per cent solids for painting and varnishing. It is compatible with linseed oils, avoids the use of more pungent solvents, and handles better than the other *Acryloid* types.

Yeffe Kimball. Some twelve years ago Yeffe Kimball began to use many of the plastic media in painting. With more one-man shows to her credit than any other living woman painter, Miss Kimball has exhibited her synthetic media paintings widely and as a result interested many artists in the possibilities of new technical means.

Miss Kimball makes most of her own plastic paints. She has a definite advantage over most artists in this project because her husband, Harvey Slatin, Ph.D., is a nuclear physicist who often advises her on chemical matters involved in making the paints. Miss Kimball mixes raw acrylic resins, pure powder pigments, plasticizers, preservatives, and stabilizers in a wide variety of recipes to achieve a vast array of properties. Some paintings are of unusually high gloss, others are completely matte, and still others combine the two. Very thin glazes and heavy impastos occur. Sometimes she adds inert clays, oil paints, and manufactured synthetic paints. Lumps of pigment may be used to give a colored stone effect. In short, Miss Kimball has taken to the synthetics as to the manner born, and her paintings are a never ending stream of exploration of the new media.

One result of her mastery of the acrylic media is *Solar Continuum* (Figure 66 and Color Plate 27, page 126) which is perhaps the first outdoor painting-in-the-round. The ten-foot-high cylindrical painting was exhibited on

Figure 65. PETALOID NO. 2, 90×84 inches, by Adolph Gottlieb, 1963. Media: *Lucite* and oil (Courtesy: the artist.)

Adolph Gottlieb likes the acrylic resin *Lucite* as the basis for a synthetic painting medium because he has not been able to duplicate with any other substance the effects it makes possible.

Gottlieb's *Petaloid No. 2* is painted on commercially prepared linen canvas that was given an over-all tone of green with his own mixture of *Lucite* 44 (his formula is on this page) oil paint, and turpentine. The priming tone was very fluid, and it brushed on easily and dried relatively fast. Oil colors and turpentine added to Gottlieb's synthetic mixture produce a medium with both viscosity and liquid flow. In this painting, these characteristics were necessary to achieve the luminous, almost oscillating orb and the bursting shape beneath it. The round shape was brushed and rubbed into form with a cloth. The bottom figure was literally flipped into configuration with a palette knife; this could not have been done with a less opaque or less viscous paint. Like the tonal underpainting, the shapes are shades and tones of green.

Most of Gottlieb's recent paintings are handled in a similar manner.

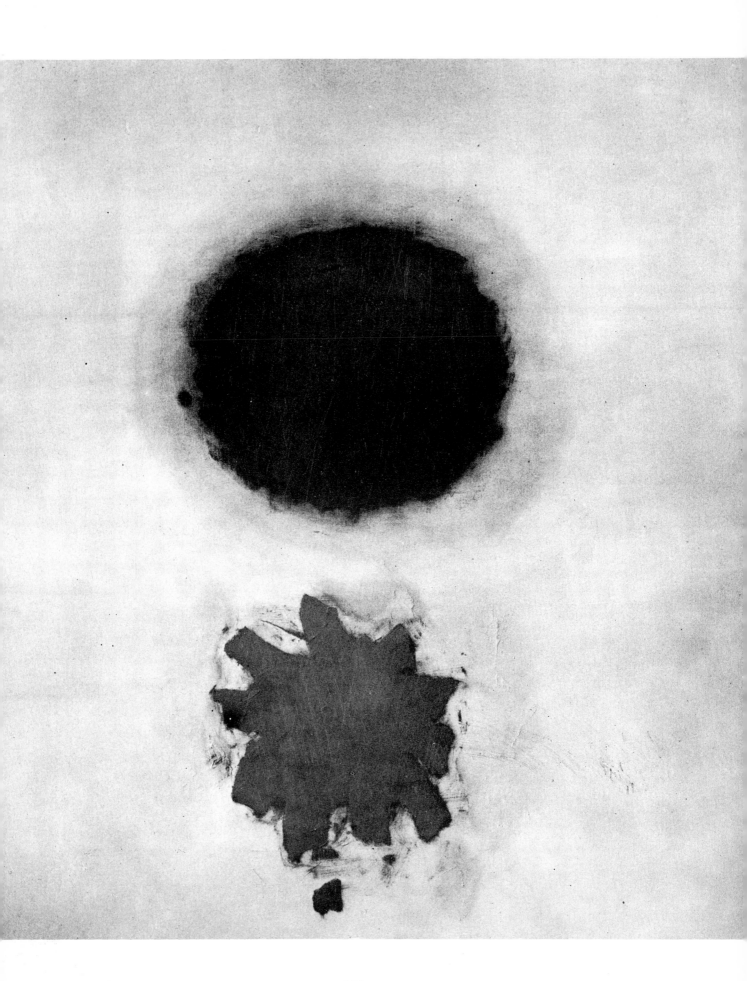

27

28

Figure 66. SOLAR CONTINUUM (detail), ca. 5 feet high, by Yeffe Kimball, 1962. Medium: Acrylic resin. (Courtesy: the artist. Photo by Marvin P. Lazarus.)

This is a detail of Color Plate 27, showing the surface quality of the acrylic resin paint. Flatness is contrasted with crater-like texture in the upper portions. The plastic, rubbery quality that can be achieved is seen in the middle impastos; below this, very fluid paint has been almost splashed onto the canvas. The same synthetic resin is capable of producing all these varied effects, depending on the additives used with the resin varnish.

the terrace of the Chrysler Museum in Provincetown, Massachusetts, for almost two years and was displayed outside the TWA Terminal at John F. Kennedy Airport in New York. The base is a specially built marine plywood drum, which the artist waterproofed with an acrylic medium she developed to achieve excellent properties of weather resistance and flexibility. Canvas, also treated with acrylic, was stretched over the drum. The painting, which almost feels like rubber to the touch, has no trace of deterioration due to weathering, including the fading effects of ultraviolet rays.

Archimedes (Figure 67) is a more conventionally shaped work (forty by thirty-two inches) which also reflects Miss Kimball's concern with themes having to do with outer space. The central vortex has great depth achieved by many layers of transparent acrylic, sometimes combined with oils, which give a reflective and three-dimensional quality that is technically amazing.

Miss Kimball buys all of her raw materials herself—including fifty and hundred pound drums of powdered pigments—and formulates her media in well ventilated Provincetown and New York City studios. Over the years she has experienced no health problems due to toxic thinners. But she and her husband fully understand the chemicals she employs, and knowledge is 90 per cent of the battle.

Color Plate 27. SOLAR CONTINUUM, 10 feet high × 4 feet in diameter, by Yeffe Kimball, 1962. Medium: Acrylic resin. (Courtesy: the artist.)

This cylindrical painting was done with acrylic resin especially formulated by Yeffe Kimball to withstand outdoor exposure. It is seen here as it was exhibited on the terrace of the Chrysler Museum, Provincetown, Massachusetts, in 1962 and 1963. The artist is seated on the museum steps.

Solar Continuum is painted on heavy linen canvas pre-treated with acrylic resin both in preparation for painting and to withstand atmospheric corrosion. The painted canvas was stretched over a specially prepared marine plywood cylindrical drum which was properly treated for water resistance and to prevent deterioration through exposure.

"The medium used in the painting," Miss Kimball explains, "comprises pure inorganic pigments which are not susceptible to corrosion nor oxidation. Ultraviolet-ray absorbers stabilized the medium to the effects of sunlight, and there was stabilization of the binder against ageing, moisture, heat, and cold. The paint was applied to the canvas by brush, by spatula, and by other means common in art. Intensity was attained by the application of several layers and the mixing of pigments."

Color Plate 28. PARADE, 18×24 inches, by Eugene Massin, 1961. Media: *Magna* and oil. (Collection: Mr. and Mrs. B. Blumberg.)

Magna was diluted with mineral spirits and used for its quick-drying characteristics as an underpainting medium for oil in this work by Eugene Massin. *Magna* was applied in an oil technique with some impasto. Oils were painted over the synthetic in heavy areas. Wet impasto was piled over and into wet impasto. The support was linen canvas.

Magna. *Magna* colors, produced by Bocour Artist's Colors, Inc., are ready-to-use paints in which pigments are already ground into an acrylic resin vehicle. Thirty-two colors, corresponding to oil colors, comprise the *Magna* line.

Magna is an excellent medium for those who want a more permanent and faster drying version of an oil paint. The cost is about the same. *Magna* colors have the same qualities and consistency as oil paints. They handle in the same manner as oils, and are relatively compatible when mixed with turpentine, linseed oil, or a special *Magna* Painting Medium. They can also be mixed with oil tube colors. *Magna* paints from the tube dry in about two hours on the painting surface. When they are mixed with the painting

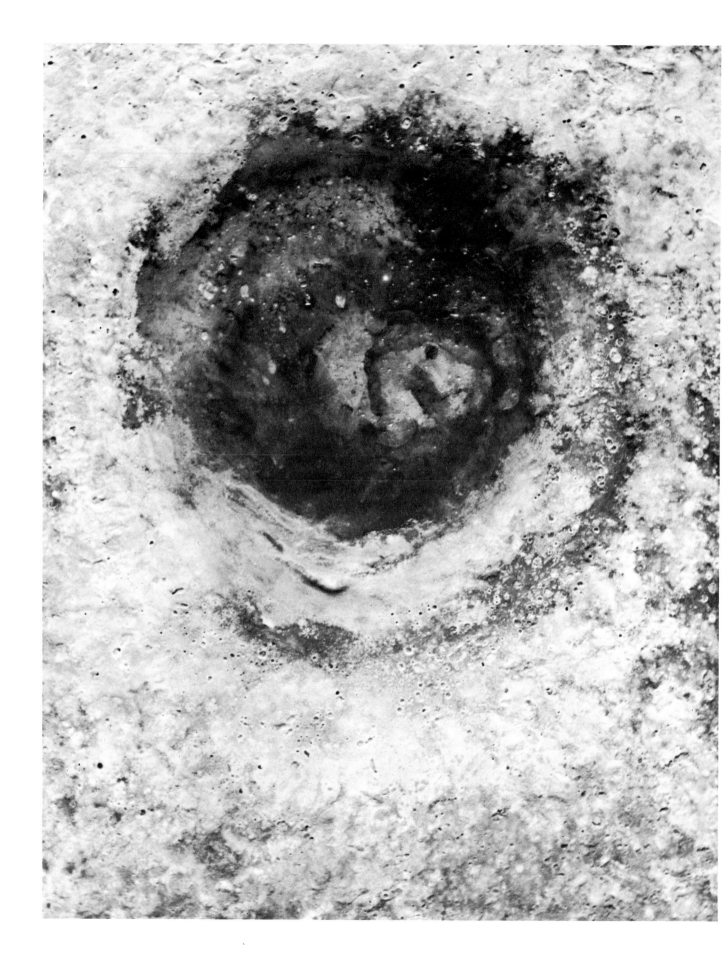

128

medium, turpentine, or mineral spirits, drying time is reduced to about one half hour.

One disadvantage with *Magna* is that it tends to pick up underlying colors, thus muddying succeeding glazes. A *Magna* varnish is suggested to coat a surface so that it will not affect succeeding layers, but this seems of questionable sureness. The varnish is made from a vinyl plastic, which will not mix with the acrylic medium, so the paint surface must be *completely* dry to the touch before the varnish can be used. If wet paint and varnish come in contact, they produce a highly unpleasant sticky substance that is very hard to clean from the brush, even with a strong solvent.

Many artists are using *Magna* to advantage. Karl Zerbe had a show of *Magna* paintings in 1959 which were generally assumed to be oils. Leo Manso uses *Magna* in a more or less direct technique. Eugene Massin employs the medium in a variety of ways— for quick underpainting, in impasto, alone, or in combination with oils. Massin states that *Magna* meets his requirements for a quick drying paint and also has an added brilliance of color and transparency which the lacquers he used in the past did not. He dilutes *Magna* with various degrees of mineral spirits to obtain controlled textures in brush strokes and impastos on linen canvas. *Parade* and *Party No. 4* (Color Plate 28, page 126, and Figure 68) are examples of his unique work with *Magna* and oils.

Alfred Leslie has used *Magna* for heroic-size portrait nudes with the detailed modeling and chiaroscuro associated with the Old Masters, superimposing fruits in pyramidal planes which project forward—suggesting the sensual rather than directly stating the erotic. These, such as *Two Ladies with Peas and Cherries*, (Figure 69), were built up with the *Magna* Medium over torn paper masking. Medium and paint were troweled on at times, with the

painting placed horizontally. When the painting was moved to a standing position, the paint would slide down the surface, leaving traceries. These figure paintings have a very high gloss and sculptural glazes feathered to exact modeling in the figures, with hard edges and crack-like lines caused by the masking.

Leslie's *Magna* paintings are done on canvas with a white lead ground. Some take seven or more months to complete. Leslie supposes that he could have used oils to do the series but he would have had to plot out the work exactly before starting, and he says he would have felt "more like a carpenter than a painter" in the process. In oil he would have had to do almost a bas relief and then paint over it, while with *Magna* the texture, surface quality, and paint and color characteristics were arrived at simultaneously. This is a profound difference, he states, since the *Magna* lent the ability to change his conception as he went along.

When Leslie first began to use *Magna* he would flood an area with the medium for heavy painting. This would dry differently in puddles and also produce separations and cracking. Now he brushes medium on sparsely and blends areas troweled on with the knife with a fan blending brush. Sometimes to obtain exact modeling and precise blendings, ten to fifteen coats of paint have to be blended with the fan.

A disadvantage that Leslie has found with *Magna* (besides its tendency to pick up underlying colors) is that it shrinks a great deal in drying and therefore does not lend itself to large areas of impasto. Once, a solid, heavy impasto eighteen by eighteen inches shrank a quarter of an inch.

Leslie employs lacquer thinners to clean his brushes and sometimes to thin the paint. He is also beginning to use the aqueous emulsions *Aqua-Tec* and *Liquitex* to speed drying time, porduce new surface qualities, and to get away from the use of toxic thinners.

Figure 67. ARCHIMEDES, 40×32 inches, by Yeffe Kimball, 1963. Media: Acrylic resin and oil. (Courtesy: the artist.)

To achieve the textural surfaces seen in this Yeffe Kimball painting, oil paints were mixed with an acrylic resin varnish in varying proportions and with different additives. Many separate layers of the medium were applied one over the other, with each layer being allowed to dry thoroughly before the next application. Parts of the painting were handled opaquely, but the central vortex is very transparent and has great depth and an inner reflection.

The unusual three-dimensional quality (the viewer gets the effect of looking through multiple stained-glass windows) would have been impossible to accomplish with the traditional media.

Figure 68. PARTY NO. 4, 18×24 inches, by Eugene Massin,
1962. Media: *Magna* and oil. (Collection: Mr. and Mrs. Jerome
Kursman.)

This painting was done on linen canvas in a manner similar to
that used for *Parade* (Color Plate 28). Massin used *Magna* as an
underpainting medium which shows through at times, comple-
menting the oil impasto. *Magna's* main advantage is as a means
of achieving quick, oil-like underpainting that permits thick
oil manipulations to continue after a relatively short drying
time.

Figure 69. TWO LADIES WITH PEAS AND CHERRIES, 66×96 inches, by Alfred Leslie, 1963. Medium: *Magna*. (Courtesy: the artist.)

Alfred Leslie says that he had four ideas in mind when he started work on a series of paintings that included *Two Ladies*: (1) He wanted the female nude to be the subject. (2) The nude would also be a portrait of a specific person. (3) He would use the "grand manner" and the detailed modeling of the Old Masters. (4) He would employ other forms such as fruits to show as little of the actual nude figure as possible, yet give the viewer the impression that he was looking at a nude figure painting.

In *Two Ladies*, the surface became a flatly treated surface of fragments. The canvas served as the first plane, with the other elements built in pyramidal planes that project forward in space from the surface.

The surface was first primed with five coats of white lead; then paper shapes were torn and applied to it with *Magna* Medium.

The impasto lines around these torn shapes were created by pulling up the edges of the paper with a knife while they were still damp, and folding them over. The cracks were the result of first piling on *Magna* paints while the painting was in a horizontal position and then placing the work vertically so the paint would slide down. The heavy, dark lines were masked out with tape. At times the tape was pulled off while the paint was wet to produce different types of feathered edges.

The faces and the fruits were modeled and blended with a fan brush over sparsely applied *Magna*. It took ten to fifteen modeling-blending-glazing processes before the desired effect was achieved. The final work has a very high gloss created by many glazes and two final coats of *Magna Medium*.

Chapter 2 / Vinyl Resin Solutions

Two types of vinyl resin can be used as the basis for artists' solution paints: vinyl acetate and vinyl chloride-acetate. They are not compatible with either oil or water but must be used as media in their own right. Handling and visual effects of vinyl paints most closely resemble the acrylic varnish solutions (Part III, Chapter 1). With the exception of *Vinylseal,* a liquid product in which vinyl acetate is dissolved in acetone, all forms of vinyl resin must be made into a resin solution and pigmented by the artist. (*Vinylseal* must be pigmented, too.) All the vinyl resins described here, including Vinylseal, are produced by Union Carbide and Carbon Corporation, New York.

Vinyl Acetate. There are two vinyl acetate resins suitable for paints: *Vinylite* AYAF and *Vinylite* AYAT. Both come in crystal-like form. Preparing a paint medium from the vinyl acetates is more difficult than with other synthetic resins. First, dissolve 100 grams of either resin in 250 cubic centimeters of acetone. When the resin is dissolved, add 250 to 500 cubic centimeters of denatured alcohol (a stabilizer for the medium as well as a thinner), according to the consistency desired. To this add 20 cubic centimeters each of Butanol (a blending agent) and Carbitol (a retarder). These

are also products of Union Carbide.

The resulting medium will keep for several months in tightly closed containers. The mixing of pigments with the medium is the same as for the acrylic solutions.

Vinyl acetate paints handle in the same manner as the acrylic varnish solutions which use toluene and xylene as solvents: they dry very fast, dissolve and muddy underlying layers of paint if not applied quickly, and dry to a gloss sheen. The gloss can be reduced by the addition of inert powders such as celite or talc. The addition of pigments reduces the gloss somewhat, too.

Vinyl acetate paints are thinned with alcohol and brushes are cleaned with alcohol. Alcohol also produces a transparent glaze, if enough is added to the paints.

Vinyl acetate is very flexible and, even when painted on paper, will not produce cracks or wrinkles if the support is rolled. The paints should not be used on oily or greasy surfaces. Any other materials, including metals, leathers, and plastics, may be employed as supports.

Unpigmented vinyl acetate medium makes an excellent glue for almost any material. It can also be used as a protective coating for paintings, sculptures, and other objects, including craft work, books, pottery, etc. A clear

gloss surface results, which can be washed.

Vinyl acetate is not recommended for exterior use because water will affect it over long periods of time.

My personal opinion of vinyl acetate is that the medium is too difficult to prepare, is something of a safety and health hazard because of the use of acetone (which not only is highly toxic but also has a low flash point, thereby making it liable to explode on contact with intense heat or flame), and has no advantages over the other synthetic media except for being an excellent adhesive and protective coating.

Vinyl Chloride-Acetate. Easier to prepare and advantageous for outdoor mural painting are the vinyl chloride-acetate resins which are called *Vinylite* VMCH and *Vinylite* VYHH. Either of these white powders can be dissolved in methyl isobutyl ketone. Methyl isobutyl ketone is a highly toxic solvent and the artist should handle it with care; do not breathe the vapors and do not let it come into prolonged contact with the skin (wear rubber gloves when handling it). The mixture to form a solution medium should be about one part resin to three parts ketone measured by volume. Proportions can be varied to produce the desired quality of vehicle. No other additives are necessary.

This medium again is handled in the same manner as the other resin solutions discussed. The range of pigments and manner of mixing are the same as with other artist-mixed paints. Thinning and cleaning of vinyl chloride-acetate is done with methyl isobutyl ketone.

For exact formulas and detailed descriptions of how to apply vinyl acetates and vinyl chloride-acetates, José Gutiérrez' book, *From Fresco to Plastics,* should be consulted. One example he describes of an outdoor mural in Mexico City painted with vinyl chloride-acetate testifies to this medium's applicability for outdoor use. The mural wall of concrete, faces south and gets at least seven hours of sunshine a day. After eleven years of weathering the only color change that occurred was the darkening of the chrome green.

(Despite the many examples in this book of outdoor murals painted in various synthetic media with remarkable durability, there is still no known permanent outdoor paint. All will show the effects of weathering in time. The synthetic media are better than those used in the past, but the final answer has not yet been found.)

Chapter 3 / Lacquers

Synthetic lacquers have probably been used for fine arts purposes longer than any other synthetic paint, at least in an experimental way. The synthetic lacquers generally available today, however, are dubious as to durability, and at their present stage of development, I do not recommend them as an outstanding medium for painting. Some producers are now perfecting acrylic lacquers that would offer greater durability, and some of these acrylic lacquers will be available in the near future.

Natural lacquer, derived from the sap of a variety of the sumac tree (*Rhus verniciflus*), was used as early as 1027 B.C. in China. First used to coat bowls and utensils, it eventually came to be employed as a painting medium. Natural lacquer is almost impossible to obtain today in the Western world because it is produced only for local use in China, Japan, India, and several other countries in the Far East.

Synthetic lacquers, in the general sense, are paints which dry quickly by evaporation of a solvent to a hard gloss finish that resembles natural, Oriental lacquers. This general definition would include the synthetic resin paints already discussed, so lacquers in this chapter are limited to clear lacquers sold as such, and to those commercial,

pigmented lines which are produced by manufacturers for industrial coatings such as automobile finishes. These may be used as a painting medium.

Early synthetic lacquers contained a cellulose called pyroxylin (or nitrocellulose), but this has severe drawbacks for painting because nitrocellulose decomposes with time, does not produce a satisfactory film, and is relatively inflexible. (In making nitrocellulose the cellulose molecule is considerably degraded, broken down, and this leaves a tendency to break down further; nitric acid is formed, which in traces turns the film brown and in greater quantity destroys the film and everything with which it is in contact. This process may take ten or twenty years, or more, depending on the environment.)

Today, acrylic resins are used in many lacquers. Sometimes they are combined with nitrocellulose, and sometimes with alkyd resins, but the best lacquer for fine arts purposes is one that is based on pure acrylic resins. Do not buy a product containing nitrocellulose (pyroxylin) for fine arts work.

The artist can buy clear lacquer solutions and grind in his own pigments, or he can purchase pigmented lacquers. Lacquers handle similarly to the acrylic solutions discussed in Part III, Chapter 1. Lacquer Thinner is used as the

thinning agent and is also used for all cleaning of palette, brushes, etc. Lacquers are resoluble in lacquer thinner at all times. Lacquers are not compatible with water or oil and should never be used with or painted over water or oil media.

Lacquer Thinner is toxic, and, when used lavishly together with the thinner already in the formulated lacquer solutions, presents the danger of over-inhalation of the vapors. If fumes are strong enough to smell when entering the studio, there is not enough ventilation. The studio should be equipped with large exhaust fans so that fresh air is always circulated. The thinner is also highly flammable.

The main reason that artists use lacquer is its fast drying time. It will dry to the touch in two to five minutes and can be painted over at that time. Because of their speed in drying, lacquers have to be handled with quickness and sureness. This may present some difficulties at first, but as experience increases, it is usually found to be an advantage rather than a hindrance. The painter will soon find he is more sure of his ability to "put something down" than he ever was before. If desired, drying time can be slowed down by DuPont Super Retarder or other retarders used sparingly with the thinner.

Lacquers should ideally be used on a rigid surface because most lacquers now available have a tendency to become brittle. Masonite, either tempered or untempered, is perhaps the best. If a surface such as paper, canvas, or fabric is desired, these can be glued to the Masonite with clear lacquer. No priming or prepared ground is necessary with lacquers. Paper is also a good surface to work on as long as the lacquer is not applied thickly. Canvas, on the other hand, should never be used without a rigid backing, because its flexibility may crack the paint surface.

Automobile lacquers dry to a very high gloss when used undiluted. When thinned to a wash consistency they are semi-gloss. Gloss can also be reduced by mixing inert clay, celite, or marble dust with the paint. A "flat base" is also available for this purpose. This is a clear base similar to clear lacquer which can be mixed with the paint or applied over it as a varnish. When mixed with pigmented lacquers in any ratio over one part base to six parts paint, the flat base gives the pigment a transparent but matte quality; used as a varnish it simply produces a matte surface. In any mixture under one to six, the paints remain relatively opaque. With the use of flat base, gloss and matte effects can create great contrast in a painting.

When pigmented commercial brands are to be used for painting, it is important to buy the very best available. Many firms use unstable pigments in their commercial lacquers which will fade or yellow with time. It is a good idea to check with the manufacturer to determine exactly what dry pigments are used for a certain color, if they are considered stable in the medium, and if any "fillers" have been used. Even in the best quality lines, a few colors have a tendency to bleed or show through succeeding layers of paint. This is especially true of the reds.

When buying colors, ask for *tinting lacquers*, not *spray lacquers*. The latter have been thinned too much for use in brush painting and the pigment thus overdispersed. If a wash of thin but intense color is desired, the paint can be thinned with a high-grade lacquer thinner. Some of the spray lacquers are useful in glazing, however; very unusual pigments are available and might be investigated by the artist for special purposes.

If there is any doubt about the permanency of a commercial lacquer color, the artist can grind his own pigments into a good clear lacquer. High-grade clear acrylic lacquer can be obtained in three densities; heavy viscosity, medium, and thin.

Florida artist Eugene Massin has been using synthetic lacquers since 1951, with excellent results. He usually uses high-grade pigmented commercial lacquers produced by Beckwith Chandler. In the studies, *Bull* (Figure 70) and *Guitar Player* (Figure 71), done on paper, Massin drew lines in

Figure 70. BULL, 18×24 inches, by Eugene Massin, 1955. Medium: Lacquer. (Collection: Dr. and Mrs. Carl Henry Davis.)

This is a study for a painting, done on paper in lacquer. Conté crayon was used to establish the design, but little can be seen of this in the finished work. Work proceeded with very thin washes of lacquer greatly cut with thinner. The semi-opaque lines and areas were then blocked in with a palette knife, some portions being re-defined or sharply cut with opaque lacquer. The technique was very direct and spontaneous, yet precisely controlled.

135

lacquer with the palette knife or in conté, and then applied large washes of lacquer thinner in watercolor consistency. Opaque lacquer is sometimes applied over the washes for reworking or to emphasize dynamic or forceful areas, and, although he has not employed the technique in our examples, on Masonite Massin sometimes achieves impastos up to a half-inch thick, using pure lacquer with no additives of any kind.

Massin's lacquer paintings on Masonite are often extremely large. For example, *The Parking Lot* (below) is four by eight feet. Thin color washes were first applied over the raw, untempered support and were followed by heavy paint. The palette knife was used to scrape out and block in areas, and to scratch in lines. Final work was done in very transparent glazes, resulting in a great feeling of depth coalescent with flat, painterly design.

It is important to remember that washes or glazing techniques with lacquers—as well as acrylic and vinyl solution paints—have to be accomplished quickly so that the underpainting does not dissolve or pick up. In my *Seated Girl* (Figure 72), the Masonite support was first scored with a knife to achieve textural lines, and many glazes, washes, and scumbles were done in a free, fast manner to complete the work.

THE PARKING LOT, 48×96 inches, by Eugene Massin, 1957. Medium: Lacquer. (Collection: Mr. and Mrs. Irving Rabinowitz.)

This large lacquer painting by Eugene Massin was painted on a sheet of untempered Masonite in Beckwith Chandler automotive lacquers. Black, tinting white, gold toner (a brown transparent color), and Ultramarine Blue were the principal colors Massin used.

Says the artist: "The first application, a direct approach, used thin washes of general colors. After the entire board was covered, a heavier lacquer was applied. Areas were scraped—I used a large painting knife—and lines were scratched across various surface areas, with the knife's edges dipped in fluid paint. I added glazes, using the transparent gold toner, and continued overpainting until the desired effect was achieved.

"The lacquer was applied without a ground, directly on Masonite. The brushes used were Harrison Fitches, ranging in size from three-quarters of an inch to two-and-a-half-inch supers. The painting knives were four-inch tapered spatulate types."

Figure 71. GUITAR PLAYER, 22×30 inches, by Eugene Massin, 1955. Media: Lacquer and Conté crayon. (Courtesy: the artist.)

Guitar Player is similar in technique to *Bull* (Figure 70), but the use of conté crayon to draw in the figure can easily be observed. All the hard, black lines, as well as the textural grays, are conté. Broad washes established the major areas and blended some of the soft conté. Whites were used in the design for emphasis and clarity. The white strings of the guitar, for example, were drawn in thinned lacquer with the palette knife.

Because lacquer dries so fast, it does not muddy conté crayon or cause it to blur when used over it, unless the conté is actually scrubbed with the brush.

Figure 72. SEATED GIRL, 24×34 inches, by Russell Woody, 1959–60. Medium: Lacquer.

For this work in lacquer, a Masonite panel was scored with a mat knife, the basic design being worked out by a cut-and-slash method before any paint was applied. The lines seen in the illustration were created by the slight raised burr that resulted from this cutting and slashing. Multiple washes and glazes of lacquer were painted over the linear structure. Most colors were greatly diluted with thinner. No opaque paints were used.

Chapter 4 / Ethyl Silicate

Ethyl silicate is the only synthetic medium discussed in this book which the artist *should not* use. It has no relation to the other synthetics in chemical makeup or drying properties. The only reason for this very short chapter on the medium is to warn the artist of its disadvantages.

Ethyl silicate is a colorless liquid which must be exactly formulated by the artist. It includes denatured alcohol and hydrochloric acid in its formulation, and dries by a chemical action (ethyl silicate is hydrolyzed by water to alcohol and silicic acid and, in turn, forms pure silica). Paints made with ethyl silicate are normally dry to the touch after an hour, but it takes three weeks for them to dry thoroughly and several months for the medium to turn to pure silica, its final state.

Artists have experimented with silicates since the 1930's (especially in Mexico) and some of them think highly of the silicates as a medium for murals because of their excellent adherence to such materials as plaster, brick, cement, etc. José Gutiérrez experimented with the medium and describes its use favorably in his book on mural painting, *From Fresco to Plastics*. Ralph Mayer also recommends ethyl silicate in his *The Artist's Handbook*. Some authors now writing about the synthetics have taken these recommendations — sometimes almost verbatim from the above books — and restated them, evidently without using the material, without talking with artists who have struggled with the medium, or without viewing the results of murals painted with ethyl silicate.

One of the most often reproduced murals in ethyl silicate is the *National Allegory* by the great Mexican muralist, José Clemente Orozco, in the Escuela Normal para Maestros, Mexico City. This mural was painted in 1947 in the outdoor theater of the teacher's school and serves as the back wall of the stage. It incorporated huge incised lines in the concrete wall and large strips of bright metal, as well as the ethyl silicate paints. When I saw the work in 1959 it was in a state of complete deterioration; very little of the paint could be seen and the incised lines and metal were only things left of the definitive design. This mural is usually reproduced in its original condition to support the misdirected statements of ethyl silicate advocates.

The deterioration of works done with ethyl silicate is not necessarily due to the medium itself, but caused by the severe handicaps the medium places on the artist in formulation and execution which the artist finds difficult to follow. These are:

1. Ethyl silicate must be exactly formulated by the artist. A variance in measuring of a few cubic centimeters or a slight variance in the mixing procedure will cause the medium to fail.

2. Laboratory equipment, such as cylindrical measuring glasses, beakers, glass rods and enamel funnels, is necessary.

3. The medium has to be mixed each week; after this time the medium begins to turn to a useless gel, even if kept in airtight glass jars.

4. One coat of ethyl silicate paint should never be painted over another or there is the danger it will flake off. Each coat of paint must be scraped off before an overcoat will make a proper bond. (This happened in the Orozco mural.)

5. Pigments have to be mixed with the medium somewhat stronger than intended because the colors lower in intensity on drying

6. Ethyl silicate will sometimes cloud the more transparent pigments.

7. Reoccuring, whitish bubbles sometimes appear on the paint surface (especially on masonry supports) and these have to be washed off periodically with soap and water.

8. A porous material must always be used as a support, and masonry surfaces must be neutralized with hydrochloric acid.

9. Inert clays have to be mixed with ethyl silicate to give it body and to reduce its higher gloss.

Because of these handicaps and because almost all artists I have talked with who have used the medium have met with minor disasters, I would never recommend ethyl silicate as a fine arts medium.

Conclusion

A comparison of oil and other traditional media with the synthetic media outlined in this book proves that the new media available to the artist are superior in durability, drying time, ease in handling, and variety of visual effects. The synthetic paints should answer most of the technical problems which are inherent in the new forms of artistic expression today, as well as eliminate those problems constantly related to traditional media and its means of execution.

The synthetics are probably ten times more durable than oil, do not require the rigid rules to produce lasting work, and have remarkably shorter drying times. (The slowest drying plastic paint mentioned here requires only four hours before overpainting can be applied. The fastest drying oil I have used takes eight hours to set before additional work can be done, and this was only accomplished by the use of fast drying whites, fast drying gel, drying oils, and the omission of glazing.) Synthetics can duplicate the effects of traditional media, from watercolor through sculpture. The new visual effects possible may well open new ways of expression. A start has been made by many of the outstanding artists represented in this book as well as others not explicitly listed. If prejudice toward newness or change in media is overcome, new pictorial ideas will be forthcoming and artists will not have to follow outmoded technical rules.

I have used or investigated most of the synthetic paints available and that I think reliable—those touched on here. Of these paints I consider the acrylic emulsions the best. They are fast drying, easy to handle, can be used to produce any texture, surface or quality desired, are amazingly durable, are non-toxic, and relatively inexpensive. Their correct technical use is simple; only a few rules need be followed to produce lasting results. They give films of great strength and flexibility without the use of additives to create these properties. Correctly pigmented colors are available in both a tempera and oil-type consistency. When the emulsion is varnished with a resin solution it makes the most impervious painting medium I know.

Studio-formulated polyvinyl acetate emulsion (*Polymer Tempera*) is the least expensive of the polymer emulsions and is especially useful when large-scale works and sculpture are contemplated and expense is a prime consideration. Its only defect is its susceptibility to cold weather in a liquid state. It has greater adhesiveness but less flexibility than the acrylics; otherwise their qualities are very similar. Pigmented brands of PVA emulsion are very poor at this writing. Industrial brands of PVA emulsion can sometimes be used by the artist to advantage but should be thoroughly investigated first.

I am personally somewhat suspect of vinyl-acrylic copolymer emulsions, because they sometimes require abnormal amounts of additives and/or plasticizers which cause undesirable side effects such as cracking or high-pressure sensitivity. (I have experienced cracking in a few of the new acrylic brands, too, however—possibly because of inept formulation).

Acrylic resin solutions are probably the most permanent paint medium today. (To a lesser degree this also applies to the vinyl resin solutions.) They require studio mixing and pigment grinding procedures, however, and the artist needs to acquire experience in this. They also require toxic thinners for the most part and should be handled with extreme care. *Magna* ready-made acrylic resin colors eliminates most of these problems but has peculiarities of its own which are discussed in Part III, Chapter 1.

Lacquers and ethyl silicate are virtually dead media and are better left unexhumed. Although they served as an important historical chapter in the use of synthetics as fine arts media, their disadvantages far outweigh their advantages. Other media in this book can do the same jobs, better.

No one medium will ever offer a solution to all the problems the artist faces. The questions of creativity and new forms of expression can only be answered by the artist. It is his duty and purpose to make the medium he uses express his intentions, emotions, ideas—his whole artistic being—even if the medium consists of mud. He should therefore choose, after experimentation, a paint that will enable him to achieve his fullest expression. All this the artist has to answer for himself. This book has been written to assist the artist in that choice.

APPENDIX

PART I The New Synthetic Pigments

Few artists perhaps realize what a range of great antiquity and recent modernity they have in the colors with which they paint and which they regard as a *traditional* palette. Of the twenty-two pigments most generally used, about half (Flake White, Ivory Black, Naples Yellow, and seven Earth and Iron Oxide colors) go back to the Renaissance and before. Zinc White, Ultramarine Blue, Alizarin Crimson, Cadmium Yellow, Cobalt Blue, Cerulean Blue, Viridian, and Prussian Blue date from the eighteenth and nineteenth centuries. It is since the beginning of the twentieth century that Titanium White, Cadmium Red, and Phthalocyanine Blue and Green were discovered. None of the colors now used, with the exception of the naturally occurring prototypes of Alizarin and Ultramarine, were at the disposal of the masters of the fifteenth, sixteenth, or seventeenth centuries.

The great masters had to know their mediums intimately in order to develop the maximum in chromatic power from their limited choice of colors and also to preserve as best they could colors deficient in stability. Conversely, some of the reason for loss of interest in the technology of handling various forms of oils and resin oil varnishes was that brilliant color could be obtained with the new bright pigments without

resort to many of the time-honored technical devices.

The colored clays—Siena, Umber, Ochre, Green Earth, and Red Oxides—have always been available in many places around the globe from prehistoric times. Man learned early to roast sienas and umbers to develop the rich Burnt Siena and Burnt Umber. As far back as the Egyptians he also had fairly rich colored ores: blue from Azurite and green from Malachite (both copper ores), yellow from Orpiment (arsenic ore), bright red from Vermilion (Cinnabar-mercury ore), and a deep, rich red from the Madder root, from which the color was extracted and fixed on clay to make Madder Lake. The famed Lapis Lazuli source of natural Ultramarine Blue was not developed until the fifteenth century into its really useful form. It was then that this semi-precious jewel (mined in Afghanistan and imported through Venice) began to be refined in Europe to extract the pure colored fraction. This blue was so expensive that it was used only on contract and specified by rich patrons.

Until early in the eighteenth century the artist's palette was limited to the colors of antiquity listed above, plus Naples Yellow, a lead-antimony compound; Massicot or Litharge, yellow lead oxide; several vegetable and

animal source colors such as Carmine; and ground blue glass, Smalt.

Modern Pigments

The first truly synthetic, man-made pigment was Prussian Blue, discovered by Diesback in 1704. The development of Cobalt Blue in 1802, artificially made Ultramarine Blue in 1824, and of Viridian in 1838, changed the situation entirely in blues and greens. The mineral colors Azurite and Malachite, which had become scarce and costly, could be abandoned, and the painter could rely on man's own resources. The new pigments were also more suitable for oil painting, the mineral pigments having performed best in the lean tempera film where they were originally used. The chromatic range was also bolstered by the appearance of Cadmium Yellow in this period.

Things became even more exciting when William Perkin initiated the epoch of synthetic organic pigments with the dyestuff Mauve in 1856. Most of the chemicals used to make this and other such colors that followed were based on products of the destructive distillation of coal, and hence were called "coal tar" or "aniline" colors. Unfortunately these early organic colors were mostly lacking in light-fastness or permanence. However, artists took them up with enthusiasm and disaster followed. It was in this way that the stigma of "aniline," "coal tar," or "dye" color arose to designate dangerous colors deficient in the permanency requisite for serious painting. Indeed most of those developed in the nineteenth century were deficient: but among those that appeared at an early date was the exact synthetically made reproduction of Madder—Alizarin, same as the natural material, but more pure. We were at least doing as well as nature and a bit better.

Although the naturally occurring mineral colors were quite stable, similar ones made artificially occasionally were not. Verdigris, used over quite a period, was not only tricky but poisonous. Ultramarine could go "sick" (turn gray) in time in the wrong kind of oil film. Under conditions more rigorous than those a protected painting enjoys, what is regarded as "completely permanent" does not necessarily hold up. Given strong enough sunlight, everything eventually breaks down to its basic, simplest, most stable form. So-called "mineral" or inorganic pigments with the exception of the simplest oxides and silicates (earths) will do this in time as well as the organic colors (defined as compounds of carbon). Like everything else on this earth, color permanency is a relative thing and dependent on environment.

The New Era

Two of our most used mineral type colors, Cadmium Red and Titanium White, along with minor synthetic mineral pigments like Manganese Blue and Manganese Violet, date from 1900. But the turning point in color chemistry, the important beginning of the modern epoch, has occurred in the last generation. This was the discovery of the Phthalocyanines in 1928 and their appearance as well developed, commercially available pigments in 1935.

Phthalocyanine Colors. Phthalocyanine blues and greens are organic pigments, complex and of large molecular size, but so symmetrical and tightly knit in their structure that they rival the best in mineral pigments in light resistance and stability under the most stringent and adverse conditions. They set a standard of perfection that gave exciting new impetus to color research and development. In the sum total of their useful qualities, intensive research has not improved on the Phthalocyanines for the blue and green range in the thirty-five years since.

Vat Dye Colors. Most of the valuable results arising from the reassessment of approach and methods in developing brilliant, highly lightfast pigments have occurred in the last ten years. We have possessed for some time certain textile "vat" dyes of phenomenal permanency, some so lightfast that they outlast the fabrics they color. But the form of a color that dyes cloth is not usually the form useful as a pigment. A pigment to be used in paint must be insoluble and of such a physical nature as to form fine, brilliantly reflective color particles. A vat dye is formed in the fiber of the cloth. To transform such materials to usable pigments has been difficult.

So far a few colors from the vat dye fields have come within the artist's reach. These include the more recent Thioindigo Violets, Indo (Perinone) Orange, and Dioxazine Purple. The latter, chemically known as Carbozole Dioxazine, is a deep blue violet of exceptional strength and is a valuable and unique addition in this part of the chromatic range.

Quinacridone Colors. A new class of pigments, initially worked on in Germany but brought to practical fruition by the DuPont Company, is the Quinacridone group that appeared in 1958. The first of these were in the blue-red to violet range and are in the Phthalocyanine class for lightfastness. Since then other variations have become available, reaching down into the middle red and one blossoming into a brilliant Magenta hue. Manufacturers of artist colors were not slow in including various of these Quinacridones in their lines, appearing under such trade names as *Acra, Monastral,* and *Shivastra,* and with the particular company name designation. To insure that any such proprietary named color is ac-

Color Plate 30.

63-L-25	Alizarin Crimson-a
63-L-2	Naphthol ITR Crimson-a
63-L-7	Red FGR-a
63-L-26	Quinacridone Scarlet-a
63-L-5	Red FRLL-a
63-L-8	Red FGG-a
63-L-9	Pyranthrone Scarlet-a
63-L-22	Cadmium Red-a
63-L-24	Carbazole Dioxazine-a
63-L-23	Quinacridone Magenta-a
63-L-10	Thioindigo Violet-a
63-L-16	Perinone Orange-a
63-L-20	Yellow HR
63-L-13	Azo Anisidide Yellow-a
63-L-12	Hansa Yellow G-a
63-L-19	Yellow NCG-a
57-V-20	Alizarin Crimson-o
57-C-1	Cadmium-Barium Red-o
57-C-6	C.P. Cadmium Red-o
57-C-7	Cadmium-Vermilion Red-o
57-C-12	Thioindigo Violet-o
57-W-45	Phthalocyanine Peacock-w
57-W-57	Phthalocyanine Blue-w
57-C-8	Viridian-o
57-C-9	Phthalocyanine Green-o
57-W-59	Phthalocyanine Green-w
57-W-61	Pigment Green B-w
63-L-18	Phthalocyanine Green-a
63-L-27	Metal Oxide Green-a

a — in acrylic polymer vehicle
o — in oil vehicle
w — in water color vehicle

Exterior Exposure Test on concrete slab of acrylic polymer emulsion paints.

Exposure Test Panels of Organic Synthetic Pigments.

Views of exposure racks where accelerated tests are made for resistance to fading of colors and resistance to embrittlement and cracking of vehicles.

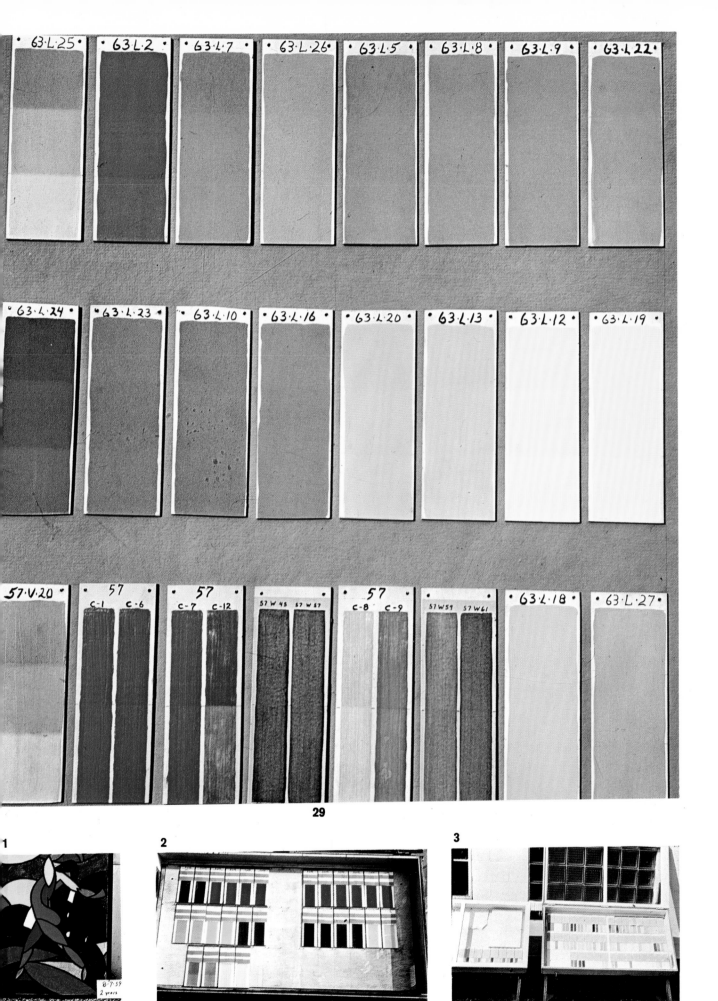

tually a Quinacridone, the artist should look to see that it is subtitled "Quinacridone" under the color name and that it is specified as "Linear Quinacridone," its full descriptive name, in a statement of pigment composition.

Azo Colors. By far the most numerous general class of bright organic colors in general industrial use is the *Azo* group. This includes most of the bright reds and yellows used in printing inks and ordinary paints. One dependable pigment class in this Azo category is the Hansa group, used for some years now by artists as a dependable color. But most Azos were not this reliable and it is in the Azos that the greatest number of improved pigments has come in the last ten years.

By reexamining methods of synthesis and devising whole new ways of putting these complicated chemical molecules together, color chemists have found ways to increase the molecular weight from the 600 region to around 1500. Many of these are doubled molecules, connecting together two of what could previously only be made as one molecule. Hence the name "Diazo" colors, also called *Azo Condensation* products.

In many cases, the making of much larger and balanced chemical units has made for more stable colors, both chemically and in light resistance. To give an idea of how much effort color manufacturers have put into such a search, over 10,000 different Azo compounds have been synthesized and tested in the last ten years. Gaertner, in his paper mentioned below, lists twenty-three greatly improved, or "high grade," Azo pigments resulting.

Two very thorough and excellent surveys of these new synthetic pigments have been published: "Exposure Studies of Organic Pigments in Paint Systems," by Vincent C. Vesce, *Official Digest*, December 1959, Vol. 31, No. 419; and "Modern Chemistry of Organic Pigments," by H. Gaertner, *Journal of the Oil and Colour Chemists' Association*, 1963, No. 1, 13—44. Both authors are leading color research chemists, Vesce in the United States, Gaertner in Switzerland. Most of the data on new synthetic pigments in this chapter is from these two sources and

from the testing done in artists' media by the research laboratory of Permanent Pigments Inc.

Physical Properties

Before discussing and examining the individual colors, it would be well to consider some of the general physical properties of synthetic organic pigments and how they adapt to artists' media and use. As was previously mentioned, people have the idea that organic colors are still "coal tar" or "aniline" colors, meaning unstable and unreliable materials. These terms are utterly obsolete and should be completely forgotten. There are organic colors or pigments that are not resistant to light but are very brilliant and used for printing inks and other purposes that do not require sustained resistance to sunlight. There are also many that are good enough for ordinary paints when they are not diluted to tints. As tints such colors may last only a few weeks. But there are the new synthetic pigments which we have been discussing in a general manner here and which will be examined in detail following, that are in the same category of reliability as some of the best "traditional" colors such as Cadmiums and Viridian. So, although it had a legitimate basis up to a generation or so ago, the stigmatic appellation of "coal tar" and "aniline" color is completely out of date, now just an "old wife's tale."

Texture. Most mineral type pigments such as earth colors, cadmiums, Cobalt Blue, and whites are rather dense, substantial feeling materials that require relatively little medium to make a workable paint. Pure organic pigments, on the other hand, are light and fluffy, require considerable binder to wet the small particles and to provide the additional fluid to surround them and make a flowing paint. The artist is familiar with this characteristic in Alizarin Crimson.

Tinctorial Strength. On the other hand, these organic *toners* (the pure color) are usually many times as strong tinctorially and can be diluted much further without losing strength than such colors as Cadmium. For example, in order to compare Cadmium Red with

organic toner reds for exposure tests five times as much Cadmium had to be used with the same amount of Titanium to produce a tint strength at all comparable with the organic reds.

Inert Additives. In oil color such a pure organic pigment ground with oil only does not have desirable qualities for a good paint film because of the high ratio of oil to pigment. A soft film that can show excess yellowing and even wrinkling may result—one that is far too "fat.". It is actually desirable to include a proportion of dense, colorless, inert mineral pigment to make a good paint. For this purpose a paint manufacturer would use synthetically made Barium Sulfate, known as *Blanc Fixe* in the trade. Artists can use whiting or clays but these are inferior additives in an oil film. A grind of straight organic color in oil may be 60 to 70 per cent oil. Use of a moderate amount of Blanc Fixe will not perceptibly reduce the strength of the color and will bring the oil content down to a normal 25 per cent as in a Cadmium grind. In this way excessively "fat" and "lean" paints would not be mixed in painting with resulting poor paint film properties.

In synthetic media, such as the acrylic emulsion, pure synthetic organic colors need no inert pigment additions because here there is no problem of excess binder. The only limit is having the minimum amount of the binding vehicle sufficient to completely "wet" the pigment particles and completely surround them to make a coherent and flexible paint film. One can get too "lean," but not too "fat." There are virtually no problems in formulative proportions or in procedural rules during painting with synthetic mediums.

Opacity. In the matter of *opacity*, the ability of the paint to completely hide or obscure the color beneath, synthetic organic pigments do present some problems since they are inherently transparent. This means that when finely ground and with great excess of medium, as in a glaze, the color will be as clear throughout as stained glass. Even with such transparent colors, as the concentration of pigment becomes greater, the opacity or hiding power increases.

A reasonable degree of opacity with these pigments is easier to achieve in an oil grind since here greater concentration of pigment can be attained. The artist is actually used to quite a variance in opacity in his normal oil paints. For example, Cadmium Red hides even in a thinly brushed film, Cadmium Yellow shows a little through from underneath, Viridian requires a thickly brushed coating to cover, and Alizarin Crimson is almost transparent, hardly covering at all.

By comparison, the synthetic organic pigments usually are more opaque than Alizarin but not quite as much as Cadmium Yellow. Hansa Yellow, one of these synthetic organic pigments, has been common in oil color lines for some time and its opacity is characteristic of the stronger pigments we are discussing here. As the hue deepens, as with Phthalocyanine Blue and Green, the ability to hide becomes greater. Carbazole Dioxazine (Dioxazine Purple) is so strong that it is highly opaque as a straight color although it is transparent when very greatly diluted.

In the synthetic mediums the organic pigments can be concentrated to the point of semi-opacity. There is no necessity of adding inerts because a tough film is formed at all pigment concentrations. Since one can overpaint in almost a matter of minutes with synthetic mediums and thick coatings present no hazard for lasting properties, inadequate opacity can be corrected by additional coats.

One of the greatest advantages of the beautiful and brilliant chromatic values of the synthetic organic colors is that in synthetic mediums the transparency can yield unequalled glazes. When color is thinned with medium to a completely transparent state, light penetrates down into the layers of glazes and is reflected back with exceptional brilliance. By varying both the concentration of the color and the thickness of the glazes, the artist has complete control of his color effects.

Grinding Organic Toners

In trying to grind his own colors with synthetic organic pigments the artist has a real problem. The fine particles of pigment are very difficult to "wet," the agglomerates (lumps of stuck-together particles) almost impossible to break up by hand. Paint mixing and grinding machinery, plus the proper additives (which can be specific for each pigment) for wetting and for emulsion stability, are virtually mandatory for making a good paint. Besides, the artist will find it difficult, if not impossible, at the present time to obtain these colors in the dry form. By the pound many are extremely expensive and are literally so messy to handle, being extremely strong and tending to fly into the air, that artists' material suppliers will not want to pack them in small containers. Being new, many are covered by patents and made only by one or a few licensed pigment manufacturers and are available only to the industrial paint maker.

Why New Colors Are Important

Why should the artist be concerned with more colors when he has a fairly adequate palette now? (After all, there are fifty to one hundred colors listed in oil color lines.) There are several reasons:

First, the colors we have been using are simply the best we have had up to now. Many are used mostly because of habit, not because there are not better ones both in chromatic value and reliability. Manufacturers know this, but they are stuck with the past list their artist users continue to demand.

Second, many of the new synthetic pigments will broaden and enhance the chromatic range, particularly where glazes and transparent use are required in new techniques made possible by the synthetic mediums.

Third, it may shortly become urgent to replace traditional colors. Synthetic organic pigments can be made in limitless quantities because the organic chemicals from which they derive can be synthesized from a wide variety of raw materials abundant everywhere. Pigments that depend on a limited supply of metal ore can go the same way as the natural ore colors Azurite and Malachite which eventually became scarce and expensive. Such a situation is developing now with the Cadmium Yellows and Reds. Cadmium metal is only found as a minor fraction in certain lead and zinc ores. Hence our supply of Cadmium is entirely dependent on how much lead and zinc are being mined and from which mines. When a new use for Cadmium develops, such as the recent Nickel-Cadmium rechargeable batteries, the demand becomes greater than the supply. In 1963 ten million pounds of Cadmium were produced and twelve millions used, the extra coming from a Government stockpile. The result was a 66 per cent increase in metal cost and four increases in pigment cost during the year plus constantly threatened material shortage. So it is well to investigate other bright yellows and reds and have them established as replacements.

Economy is a fourth compelling reason. Although very few of the reliable synthetic organic pigments are really cheap and many are very expensive, most are quite strong and need be used in much lower concentration in the grind than mineral type pigments. In the most concentrated grind, the net volume of organic pigment that can be included is one-fourth of that possible with Cadmium pigment (closer to one-eighth by weight) and the organic pigment grind will be stronger. As a result the most expensive synthetic organic pigments, costing five to ten times as much per pound as Cadmium Reds can be offered as a finished paint in the same current price range. By diluting the grind to "normal" strength for practical use, even economy price colors of high quality and permanence can be offered.

Permanency

Permanency, the ability of a color to last for centuries without change, is a primary requirement to the fine artist. A discussion of testing for permanency, for resistance to fading, is given at the end of this chapter. The drastic methods used for accelerated testing make permanency or lightfastness a relative matter in all but the simplest end product materials. What is meant by "end product" are the metal oxides and silicates (whites, earth colors, Cobalt and Cerulean blues, Chromium Oxide green, Venetian Red, Mars colors, etc.) that are at the end of the line for chemical reaction, are down to the simplest result of decomposition. Cadmium sulfides (yellow) can oxidize to colorless cadmium sulfate. Viridian, which holds combined water, can lose that water under conditions of accelerated testing and its color as well.

Let us first look at the results of actual sunlight exposure tests illustrated on page 143. On these test panels the color pigment is reduced with fifty times as much Titanium White pigment by volume in the case of the "63-" series. Total exposure was 600 hours summer sunlight under single thickness glass at a forty-five degree angle to the vertical, facing south. The upper two-thirds of the color was covered by two separate pieces, the bottom third being left exposed. After 300 hours the lower (middle) cover was removed and exposure continued for another 300 hours in sunlight. Thus the lower third was exposed 600 hours, the middle 300 hours, while the upper third had no sun exposure. In this way direct comparison can be made.

The 57-C and 57-W panels are from a 1957 exposure series and show 600 hours exposure on the lower half of the color stripe, 300 hours on the upper half. The 57-V-20 was a 1957 test formulation but exposed with the 1963 panels to correlate the degree of fading. In the 63-L-25 and 57-V-20 panels we have controls to relate the exposure to other tests at other times by comparison of the fading of Alizarin Crimson each time and to the other panels.

Fading results on pigments in accelerated tests will vary with the medium for several reasons. If the pigment is one susceptible to oxidation in oil paint the effect of the oxidation of the disintegrating oil film will cause greater fading to show than when the pigment is in an acrylic film under the same exaggerated conditions. The kind of white, whether Zinc or Titanium, the rigors of widely changing temperatures and humidity, are also major factors. It is these extraordinary environmental conditions, rather than any protective value the binder has, that will cause color fading of different rates between one medium and another and one test and another.

In making an exposure test, it is necessary always to have a "control" panel, a standard duplicate used in all the tests in order to compare these varia-tions. The amount of fading will fall within a limited range and we can judge, consequently, what the general category is to which a pigment belongs—whether it is in the same range as Cadmium or Viridian or whether it justifies rejection as being no better than Alizarin (Madder Lake).

Minor fading in an accelerated test, as will be discussed later, does not mean that a pigment will show fading under the normal conditions to which a painting is exposed. There is no actual relation other than if it will stand as much abuse as well as known permanent colors, it can reasonably be expected to perform as well under normal condi-

Terminology Used in Listing Pigments

So the reader will know what the degree of permanency is that these new pigments exhibit in accelerated testing, we will relate them to the change showed by familiar colors. These are ranges, rather than the precise values actually measured, since fading varies with the conditions and the test.

Permanency Group (A)—in a class with Cadmiums, Viridian, and Phthalocyanine Blue and Green.
Permanency Group (B)—more change than (A) and in the Hansa Yellow range. About three times as good as Alizarin.
Permanency Group (C)—range between (B) and Alizarin.

Where results vary between one group and the next in different tests the classification is given as A/B or B/C. These classifications are factual, taken from actual tests, not a matter of "opinion" as has often been the case with past listings of permanency.
The source of information on the permanency data is indicated as follows:
P—Permanent Pigments exposure test studies
V—Exposure test data given by Vesce
G—Listed by Gaertner
M—Pigment manufacturer's data
The paint binder or vehicle used in the tests are abbreviated as follows:
a—acrylic polymer emulsion binder
o—oil color
w—watercolor

Naming

Next in importance to the reliability of the pigment itself is the ability of the artist to identify it on the manufacturer's label. Obviously with these complex organic pigments the proper names are too long, too unpronounceable, to be used for label names. Without a guaranteed statement of composition somewhere on the label, however, the artist cannot be certain what the pigment is. We suggest that the simplest way to identify the pigment in the case of these synthetic organic pigments is to use what is known as the *Color Index Name*, at least in the statement of composition. This suggestion is made here for the first time and it will, if followed, take years to accomplish as common practice in labeling.

The Color Index Name is given a new color by The Textile Institute after the identity is disclosed and the reliable commercial use has been established. The Color Index Name is individual and specific for each particular kind of pigment. There is also a Color Index Number but this usually has five digits and would be more confusing and difficult to identify. An example of a Color Index Name is *Pigment Red 83* for Alizarin Crimson.

Names used by pigment manufacturers are frequently wholly proprietary and provide no indication as to the identity of the pigment. In the following listing we use the specific chemical name where possible, otherwise the most used trade designation. Even here the Color Index Name is necessary for positive identification, although in some cases, as with those Linear Quinacridones pioneered by DuPont, there is not yet a Color Index Name available.

Testing for Permanency

The individual who wishes to test permanency himself and does not have the facilities of a paint laboratory and the requisite technical background, can make only crude and perfunctory tests. He can make a tint of the color with white, paint it on a panel and, after it is dry, expose it in a window (but not against the glass) facing south. Part

SYNTHETIC ORGANIC PIGMENTS OF ACCEPTABLE PERMANENCY

PIGMENT	TYPE	SOURCE REFERENCE AND TEST MEDIUM	PERMANENCY GROUP	COLOR INDEX NAME
YELLOWS – in order from greenish to reddish hues				
GREEN GOLD	Nickel Azo	V, G	A	Pigment Green 10
HANSA YELLOW IOG	Azo	Po, V	A	Pigment Yellow 3
YELLOW NCG	Diazo	Pa	A	Pigment Yellow 16
HANSA YELLOW G	Azo	Pa, V	B	Pigment Yellow 1
AZO ANISIDIDE YELLOW	Azo	Pa	A/B	Pigment Yellow 74
ANTHRAPYRIMIDINE YELLOW	Anthraquinone	V, G, M	A	Vat Yellow 20
FLAVANTHRONE YELLOW	Anthraquinone	V, G, M	A/B	Vat Yellow 1
HANSA YELLOW R	Azo	Pw, M	A/B	Pigment Yellow 6 and 10
HANSA YELLOW RN	Azo	V, M	A	Pigment Yellow 65
YELLOW HR	Diazo	Pa, V, G	A/B	Pigment Yellow 83
ORANGES – in order of deeper hues				
HANSA ORANGE	Azo	V, M	A/B	Pigment Orange 1
PERINONE ORANGE	Perinone	Pa, V, G	A	Vat Orange 7
ANTHRATHRONE ORANGE	Anthraquinone	Pa, V, G	A	Vat Orange 3
REDS – in order of yellow reds to blue reds				
RED FGG	Azo	Pa	A	Pigment Red 148
RED FRLL	Azo	Pa	A	Pigment Red 9
QUINACRIDONE SCARLET	Linear Quinacridone	Pa, V, G	A	DuPont patent
RED FGR	Azo	Pa, V	A	Pigment Red 112
PYRANTHRONE SCARLET	Anthraquinone	Pa, V	A	Vat Orange 4
PERYLENE VERMILLION	Perylene	V, G, M	B	Pigment Red 123
PERYLENE RED	Perylene	V, G, M	A	Pigment Red 29
QUINACRIDONE RED	Linear Quinacridone	Pa, V, G	A	DuPont patent
QUINACRIDONE CRIMSON	Linear Quinacridone	Pa, V, G	A	DuPont patent
NAPHTHOL ITR CRIMSON	Arylamide Azo	Pa, V	B	Pigment Red 5
ALIZARIN CRIMSON	Madder Lake	Pa & o, V	C–	Pigment Red 83
CARMINE FBB	Azo	Pa	B	Pigment Red 146
PERYLENE MAROON	Perylene	G, M	A	Vat Red 23
QUINACRIDONE MAGENTA	Linear Quinacridone	Pa, V, G	A	Pigment Red 122
THIOINDIGO VIOLET	Thioindigo	Pa, V, G	A	Pigment Red 87
THIOINDIGO BORDEAUX	Thioindigo	V, G	A	Pigment Red 88
VIOLETS – in order from reddish to bluish hues				
QUINACRIDONE VIOLET	Linear Quinacridone	Pa, V, G	A	Pigment Violet 19
ISO VIOLANTHRONE VIOLET	Anthraquinone	V, G	A	Vat Violet 1
DIOXAZINE PURPLE	Carbazole Dioxazine	Pa & o, V, G	A/B	Pigment Violet 24
BLUES – in order from greener to redder hues				
PHTHALOCYANINE PEACOCK	Metal free Phthalocyanine	Pa & o, V, G	A/B	Pigment Blue 16
PHTHALOCYANINE BLUE	Phthalocyanine	Pa, o & w, V, G	A	Pigment Blue 15
INDANTHRONE BLUE	Anthraquinone	V, G	A	Vat Blue 4

SYNTHETIC ORGANIC PIGMENTS OF ACCEPTABLE PERMANENCY

PIGMENT	TYPE	SOURCE REFERENCE AND TEST MEDIUM	PERMANENCY GROUP	COLOR INDEX NAME
INDANTHRONE BLUE, REDDISH	Anthraquinone	V, G	A	Vat Blue 6
GREENS – in order from yellow to bluer hues GREEN GOLD – see Yellows				
PIGMENT GREEN B	Ferric Nitroso Betanaphthol	Pw, V	B/C	Pigment Green 8
PHTHALOCYANINE GREEN, YELLOWISH	Phthalocyanine	Pa, V, G	A	Pigment Green 36
PHTHALOCYANINE GREEN, BLUISH	Phthalocyanine	Pa, o, w, V, G	A	Pigment Green 7
COMPARISON MINERAL TYPE (INORGANIC) PIGMENTS CADMIUM RED	Cadmium-Barium Seleno Sulfide	Pa, o	A	Pigment Red 108
CADMIUM RED, C.P.	Cadmium Seleno Sulfide	Po	A/B	Pigment Red 108
VIRIDIAN	Hydrated Chromium Oxide	Po	A/B	Pigment Green 18

should be tightly covered to compare with the exposed portion after exposure. In six months or more of such exposure he may be able to know something about the tendency of the color to fade in strong light. The vehicle used should be one that will not darken in the covered part such as acrylic binder. A tint of Alizarin exposed at the same time will give an idea of comparative lightfastness.

The artist can depend on the manufacturer of his paint *if* the color is labeled so that there is no question of the real identity of the pigment. Abuse of the term "permanent" on labels has made the word meaningless if it is used in describing composition without specifically naming the pigment invol-ved, in which event it is obviously being used for evasion. Proprietary names are justifiable where the chemical name is unwieldy, but only if there is also true identification elsewhere on the label. Unfortunately the artists' materials industry generally has made no attempt to keep pace with the more technically advanced fields which publish actual test data to back up claims about materials. The promotional Hollywoodisms that emanate do not create fact. The kindest thing that can be said is that opinion about what is suitable for a lasting artist's color varies among manufacturers.

So, what tests have we to rely on? The pigment manufacturer frequently gives a rough rating of lightfastness which may or may not be applicable to the use in artists' colors. Even published data in the general paint field is far from comprehensive with the exception of the extensive and systematic work by Vesce referred to previously. House paint and industrial paint makers do test their colors thoroughly, but they do it in the particular kinds of paints they make and for the specific purposes for which those paints are intended. This kind of testing is for their own information.

For a test to mean anything it must be done in the mediums the artist uses and in the way he uses the color. The whole list of artists' colors available at the time was tested by the WPA Massachusetts Art Project in the 1930's and the resultant list of pigments considered reliable published as the Commercial Standard CS98-42, Artists Oil Paints. These tests were performed by exposing *full strength* paint-outs of the oil colors to the sun, protected by glass. Although there is no quarrel with the resultant conservative list, or the more recent one in the 1962 revision, CS98-62, the author contends that testing color at full strength is inadequate and literally irrelevant.

For a color to be fully reliable to the artist, it must be dependable under all conditions in which the artist uses it. How much painting is done in straight, full strength color? In achieving his desired chromatic value, the painter will mix and, more likely than not, attain just the right result by a "touch" of a modifying color, quite likely with a complementary hue. If this slight addition of color that alters the whole value of the mix were to fade, the entire color effect is lost. In other words, we are constantly concerned with very diluted tints. It makes no difference whether the major color is white or not.

The resistance that colors have to light is highly dependent on their concentration. The more a color is diluted, the more susceptible it is to fading. Obviously testing full strength colors gives us no answers since there are many colors that will hold up a year or more at full strength in the sun but will fade out completely at the same exposure in a few weeks when diluted. For commercial and industrial purposes colors are always tested greatly diluted.

Still, how is one to know whether a color will last ten, twenty, or two hundred years? We really do not, projecting time either way. We assume colors that look good now that were painted one hundred or four hundred years ago have not changed. Obviously there has been no major change or the colors would not look right. But we have no absolute comparison to make with what the colors were when they were painted. Nor do we have any completely reliable means of checking a color twenty years hence since we wouldn't know whether the comparison "standard" itself had changed. Even color reading instruments vary among themselves. We can use comparison standards and instruments to read color reliably for short term testing.

What then, does accelerated short term testing tell us? Everyone agrees that what happens to a color under very strong light will not necessarily take place to the same degree under normal indoor conditions of illumination to which a painting is usually subjected. The laboratory testing of pigments exposed to mercury arc light in the Fadeometer is not considered by color technicians as anything but a handy comparison tool that indicates no certain relation even with exposure to sunlight, much less normal conditions. For the most reliable results industry resorts to exposure to sunlight under standardized methods of test in Florida for the most accelerated tests, and in various other parts of the country, usually their plant locations.

In tests run on the same test series at Norwood, Ohio, and at Miami, Florida, for the same number of sun hours, the Norwood exposures faded 50 to 75 per cent as much as the Florida exposures, varying with the particular color. Theoretical calculation would purport to show that Florida sunlight under glass averages 2800 times as strong as indoor illumination and 4800 as great with the higher intensities of sunshine. But there is no actual relation between fading in an accelerated test and the years a color will normally last.

Since we do want to know how good new colors are, how much will tests of exposure to strong sunlight tell us? With the enormously greater light energy impinging on the color and with the wide ranges of temperature and humidity, certainly destructive changes can be initiated that might never occur in a protected room. Unless we want to wait a hundred years, when there undoubtedly will be much more attractive and better pigments available, we have to use the best short-hand we have. If we expose pigments, greatly reduced with white to make them sensitive to fading to a relatively moderate degree of sunlight, we should at least come up with ones that are indicated as reliable. That is, if they stand the tough test, they certainly can be expected to withstand the easy one of normal use. We also have the pigments with which we have had long experience to use as comparison standards to judge relative fading.

The exposure of colors, where weather resistance is not a factor, under single thickness glass at a forty-five degree angle to the vertical, facing south, is standard. Each industry has its own methods according to its products and what it is testing and the artists' color industry will have to standardize its own methods also. The important factors are to what standard degree a color is to be diluted with which standard white pigment and precisely by what method the fading of the color is to be judged.

This standardization of testing procedure requires much experimentation with different methods. The author has been engaged in this project for a number of years and there is much still to be done. One thing is certain, however, and that is that color must be read by instruments in order to have reliable data for comparison. The eye is sensitive and accurate but the "judgement" varies with each individual. All figures for fading reported herein by the author were made with the same color reading instrument and calculated for color change by the same equation for color change in NBS units given on page 258, "Color in Business, Science, and Industry", Deane B. Judd, 1952 edition.

APPENDIX

PART II Testing for New Media

How can we tell whether a new paint vehicle has the necessary stability and durability for artists' use without waiting the interminable period to have it "tested by time"? The pure acrylic emulsions have already been proven fairly well by a decade of use in outdoor house paints and for the better part of that time in artists' paints in all manner of use and application. Modern chemistry constantly produces new and astounding plastics. In what way can these new and possibly valuable materials be tested to indicate their reliability for permanent painting?

Tests such as those illustrated here will give a pretty good indication of how well vehicles will retain their elasticity and freedom from cracking and flaking—properties that insure lasting quality. The paint is applied to stretched canvas large enough to exhibit a fair degree of movement, 16×16 inches or larger. In the tests shown, high impasto pilings, the application of paint most prone to failure, are used. When the paint has dried the canvas is placed in the same outdoor sun exposure testing racks used for color testing—at a forty-five degree angle to the vertical, facing south, and protected by single thickness glass (see Appendix, Part I, Color Plate 30). The sun speeds up the hardening and embrittlement of the binder, and the

wide range of humidity and temperature produces exaggerated expansion and contraction of the canvas ground.

Figure 73 shows a canvas with very high pilings of acrylic emulsion gel and modeling paste-gel mixtures with color intermixed. The photograph was taken after seven months of exposure. The paint is in perfect condition, the only apparent change being an increased gloss due to fluxing of the surface from the heat of the sun. Of the *Liquitex* Gel we were rather certain since it is pure acrylic and has a rubbery nature. On the other hand, whether one part of gel mixed with two parts of modeling paste would take the stringent test was another question. It came through with colors flying.

A typical instance where this test proved very valuable was to evaluate an entirely new synthetic plastic developed by Permanent Pigments Inc. The object of the new material was to create a binder for highly specialized products to use with *oil* paints and where extraordinary elasticity is required to prevent eventual cracking and flaking. In quick-drying, underpainting oil whites the proportion of pigment must be abnormally high to produce the apparent fast dry (really resulting from the evaporation of solvent). Such a paint film requires a binder of extraordinary elasticity and adhesiveness.

In "oil-gel" mediums used to produce high pilings of oil paint of varying degrees of translucency there is the same necessity of great elasticity and also lack of film shrinkage with aging.

A vehicle for both purposes was achieved by polymerizing as a single chemical compound an oil-copolymer from two kinds of drying oils and four chemical monomers including various acrylics. Making a single unit, a copolymer, is entirely different from just mixing the oils and separate resins. All these ingredients were necessary to arrive at the desired properties of high binder concentration in the solvent (over twice that possible with pure acrylic resin), quick drying, nonyellowing, and permanent film flexibility. The acrylic portion contributed much of this.

Figures 74 and 75 show the results. The section of the underpainting white test illustrates what happened to two other well-known commercial underpainting whites compared with the synthetic oil-copolymer binder product. The one in the center, apparently a heavy bodied oil thinned with solvent as vehicle, really cracked up. The one on the right not only cracked, but separated from the canvas in large areas, and has a binder made with alcohol soluble resin. The drying oil-acrylic copolymer vehicle bound white

150

is shown at the left edge. Neither it, nor two accompanying variations, showed any cracking or loss of adhesion. The two that failed have been on the market for some years.

The various textured rectangles (Figure 75) are the tests of five formulative variations when this oil-acrylic copolymer is used. Each is tested with the copolymer alone and with the addition of Zinc White and Titanium White oil paints. The odd white stripe on the lower right hand corner of the canvas is *Liquitex* Gel with *Liquitex* White tested concurrently.

The artist can perform similar tests himself. The paints and/or mediums to be tested are painted on a fairly large canvas, in multiple layers, piled, and other typically extreme painting techniques. The test canvas may then be suspended inside a window facing south and just a few inches away from the glass. If the room is not too well heated, the canvas will be subjected to both extremes of temperature and humidity and there should be sufficient excess sunlight exposure to embrittle the film. Six months of such exposure will provide adequate test results.

Figure 73. Accelerated ageing tests on heavy impasto using *Liquitex* Gel (top) and *Liquitex* Gel and Modeling Paste mixtures (bottom).

Figure 74. Section of canvas of accelerated ageing test on gel mediums for oil colors. (oil-acrylic copolymer).

Figure 75. Accelerated ageing tests on canvas of oil-acrylic copolymer in five formulative variations.

GLOSSARY AND SOURCE OF MATERIALS

acetone—a strong and highly volatile solvent. See volatile thinners and solvents. Available from chemical suppliers and large drug houses.

acrylic—type of synthetic resin used in making the synthetic paints. Acrylate and methacrylate resins are made by polymerizing esters of acrylic and methacrylic acid.

Acryloid (B-44, B-72, B-82)—acrylic ester resins manufactured by Rohm and Haas Company, Philadelphia, Penn. Purchased from Rohm and Haas or its distributors in a granular state, it is dissolved in volatile thinners to make a paint solution.

Acryloid (F-10)—a soft acrylic resin already dissolved in mineral spirits. Source: same as above.

aggregates—inert materials such as sand, pebbles, Celite, etc., mixed with paints to obtain textures, greater viscosity or better bonds.

alkyd resins—synthetic resins used especially as surface coatings and with lacquer paints to give characteristics such as durability, non-yellowing, and flexibility.

álla prima—in painting, completion of a work in one sitting with paint being applied for final effect.

Aqua-Tec—acrylic emulsion paint line produced in jars and plastic squeeze bottles by Bocour Artists Colors, Inc., 552 West 52nd St., New York 19, N.Y. and available at art supply stores.

aquatint—a printing technique in which powdered rosin is applied to a metal plate, the plate is heated, and the uncovered part of the metal is etched with acid to produce grainy light and dark masses of various gradations. The plate is cleaned, warmed, inked, wiped, and printed onto paper with a special roller press to produce the aquatint.

aqueous media—any painting media with a water base.

aqueous synthetic media—water-base synthetic media which dry through the evaporation of water and become impervious to water. See polymer emulsion.

asbestine—a type of talc (hydrated magnesium silicate) used to give body to synthetics. It is an inert, fibrous pigment and will give a matte quality to gloss paints as well as slightly tint them.

bas relief—low raised sculpture relief.

binder—the material used to bind together pigment particles in a paint film. See medium.

Butanol—a blending agent to use with vinyl acetate solution paints. A product of Union Carbide Chemical Corp., 270 Park Ave., New York, N.Y., and available through its distributors.

calcium carbonate (known as "whiting") —an inert pigment used to give body and viscosity to synthetic paints as well as oil paints. Paris White is the best grade. It tints the colors and should be used by the artist only, not by manufacturers of synthetic paints. Source: pigments suppliers such as Fezandi and Sperrle, Inc., 103 Lafayette St., New York, N.Y.

Carbitol—a volatile retarder to slow down the drying time of resin solutions, especially vinyl acetate. A product of Union Carbide Chemical Corp., 270 Park Ave., New York, N.Y., and available through its distributors.

carborundum—a hard abrasive, usually black in color, and useful in its powdered or granular state as a textural additive to the synthetic paints and as a surface material for producing gray masses in collagraphy prints. Available from large building supply stores, industrial suppliers and, in some cases, from pigment suppliers.

casein—refined curd of milk which is a strong adhesive. In casein tube colors, a solution of casein in water is emulsified with various gums or oils, different with each manufacturer. Casein is too brittle to use alone as a paint binder.

Celite—a type of diatomaceous earth produced by Johns Manville, Inc., (Sales Corp.: 270 Madison Ave., New York, N.Y.) and available through large paint stores or building suppliers.

Cellosize—a chemical thickener to use with polyvinyl acetate emulsions to give more body and viscosity to the medium. A product of Union Carbide Chemical Corp., 270 Park Ave., New York, N.Y., and available through its distributors.

collage—a composition pasted together of materials such as paper, cloth, wood, found materials, etc., usually of contrasting texture and pattern.

collagraph—a print produced from a plate made by collage methods.

copal resin—a hard, natural resin that has become fossilized and is insoluble. It is fused at high temperatures so that it can be dissolved in oils and thinners to make painting mediums and varnishes.

copolymer—a polymer made by chemically combining different classes of monomers. For use in an artist's paint this should be a chemical combination of acrylic and vinyl monomers, and the term "copolymer" has that meaning in this book. Just mixing acrylic and polyvinyl polymers together does not produce a copolymer, only a mixture.

The use of "copolymer," as applied by some to the polymer made from various acrylic monomers, is not the accepted meaning in the trade. The word "copolymer" has no virtue whatever in itself, can mean any combination of any kind of monomers having no relation to suitability for use in artist's paints.

Cryla—an acrylic emulsion paint line produced in tubes by the English firm of Rowney. Available through United States distributors and art supply stores.

Darex Everflex G—an industrial polyvinyl acetate emulsion produced by W. R. Grace and Co., Dewey and Almy Chemical Division, Cambridge 40, Mass., and 225 Allwood Road, Clifton, N.J., and available through their distributors.

damar—a natural gum from a tree grown in the Malay States, bought in crystals and dissolved in turpentine (or purchased already dissolved) to make a picture varnish for oil paintings. It is a soft resin, as opposed to copal, a hard resin. Source: art supply stores.

denatured alcohol—a type of ethyl alcohol commonly sold in drug stores which can be used to increase the gloss of polyvinyl acetate paint films (see Part II, Chapter 15).

diatomaceous earth—an inert clay of light, fluffy, absorbent nature used to give body and decrease gloss in synthetic emulsions and solutions. One of the best inert fillers for this purpose. Source: pigment suppliers.

Du Pont Super Retarder—a retarder for use with lacquers to produce a slower drying time. Available at large paint stores and through industrial suppliers of Du Pont products.

emulsion—the suspension of very small drops of a liquid in another liquid or, in the case of synthetic emulsions, the suspension of minute particles of plastic resin in water. See polymer emulsion.

encaustic—pigments mixed with heated, flowing wax as a medium, painted onto a support and, when dry, fused with a hot "iron."

etching—a printing process in which a metal plate is coated with a wax or varnish ground, lines are scratched into the ground and the plate is immersed in an acid bath which bites or "etches" the exposed lines. The plate is then cleaned, inked, wiped, and printed onto paper with a special roller press to produce the etching.

Eterna—a synthetic emulsion paint line produced by Casa del Arte, Independencia, 101-C, Mexico City. It is not available in the United States.

ethyl silicate—a mural painting medium based on an organic compound of silicon. Chemical reactions change the liquid to pure silica. Ethyl silicate has to be exactly formulated by the artist. Its disadvantages are discussed in Part III, Chapter 4. For suppliers contact Union Carbide Corp., 270 Park Ave., New York, N.Y.

filler—see inert pigment, clays.

Fluoro-Veloxes—commercial art reproduction technique using fluorescent liquids for washes of black to gray which are photographed by a fluorescent screen camera.

fresco—true fresco or *buon fresco* consists of painting into a surface of freshly spread, wet plaster with water-mixed pigments. *Fresco secco* is painting onto a dry plaster wall, which has been wet with lime water, using pigments ground into an aqueous medium such as casein or the polymer emulsions. The term *fresco secco* may also be applied to any painting done on a dry plaster area.

gel medium—a thick, viscous polymer emulsion medium which dries clear. This term has been applied also to a complete variety of gelled mediums for oil painting, completely unsuitable for use with synthetic emulsions. Be sure that the medium discussed is designated for oil or water media to avoid confusion and painting problems.

gesso—traditionally, chalk or some other inert white material bound with glue to use as a white ground on rigid supports; it is not flexible. Synthetic gessos are ready-to-use liquid ground paints which have a polymer emulsion binder and can be used on any support, are flexible and non-yellowing. Synthetic gessos dry and can be painted over with any medium within 30 minutes.

glaze—transparent film of paint made by mixing a small amount of color with a large quantity of medium.

gloss medium—paint medium which dries to a highly reflective, shiney surface. "Polymer medium" and "gloss medium" are the terms used in the synthetic emulsion lines.

gouache—opaque watercolor. All pigments are used in an opaque manner as opposed to traditional transparent watercolor (aquarelle).

ground—the prepared surface upon which a painting is executed; including a "size" (to seal the surface if necessary) and "priming," which are applied to the support to give a tighter surface, a "tooth," to decrease absorbency or to increase luminosity. Grounds are not usually necessary for synthetic media unless special qualities are desired.

Hyplar—a copolymer emulsion paint line produced in jars and cans by M. Grumbacher, Inc., 460 West 34 St., New York, N.Y., and available at art supply stores.

impasto—heavy build-ups of thick paint to three-dimensional masses.

inert pigments (clays)—fine, powdery substances which do not tint or appreciably change the color of a paint when mixed with the paint for purposes of thickening or matting. Among the useful inerts are: asbestine, calcium carbonate, diatomaceous earth, Celite, marble dust, pumice, silica, talc. They can usually be obtained from industrial pigment sources (such as Fezandi and Sperrle Inc., 103 Lafayette St., New York, N.Y.) and some through drug and building suppliers. If used to excess by paint manufacturers they can become cheapeners or adulterants, but they also impart desirable qualities in specific cases.

industrial polymer emulsions—as referred to in this book: polymer emulsion produced for the industrial trade as basic mediums for house paints, industrial coatings, glues, and fine arts paints. They are unpigmented and at times require many additives to form a paint. Included are acrylics, polyvinyl acetates and copolymers.

lacquer—*traditional*: a painting medium

derived from the sap of the sumac tree found in Japan, China and the Himalayas. It dries to a hard gloss finish. Also a shellac solution made from the resinous substance secreted by a scale insect native to India. *Synthetic:* very quick drying mediums and paints produced chemically for industrial coatings and automobile finishes, which have the same hard gloss finish of traditional lacquers. Their various ingredients of cellulose compounds, synthetic resins, plasticizers, etc., are dissolved in volatile thinners and solvents. (See Part III, Chapter 3.) Source: paint stores and industrial paint houses.

lacquer thinner—a volatile thinner used to thin or dissolve lacquers. Available at most paint stores.

lean to *fat*—a painting term which is applied to oil painting, describing the rule wherein paints with least oil content (lean) should be applied before paints that contain a larger amount of oil (fat). If this rule is not followed in oil painting the paint film will crack. (See Part I, Chapter 2, *Drawbacks of the Oil Medium.*)

linseed oil—a highly purified drying oil, pressed from the seed of the flax plant and used as the medium for oil paints. Available at all art supply stores.

Liquitex—an acrylic polymer emulsion paint line produced in jars and in tubes by Permanent Pigments, Inc., 2700 Highland Ave., Norwood 12, Ohio. Available at art supply stores and through school supply houses.

Lucite—an acrylic resin produced by E. I. Du Pont de Nemours and Co., Wilmington 98, Delaware. The resin can be dissolved in volatile thinners to produce a paint medium. See Part III, Chapter 1 for various types and their uses. Small quantities are obtained from Du Pont distributors, large paint stores, or from Almac Plastics, Inc., 600 Broadway, New York 12, N.Y. For technical information write: E. I. Du Pont de Nemours and Co., 350 Fifth Ave., New York 1, N.Y.

Luzitron—an acrylic resin solution sold as a paint medium and varnish by José Gutiérrez, Calle Tigre No. 24, Mexico 12, D.F. (See *Politec.*)

Magna—an acrylic resin-solution paint line, pigmented and sold in standard artist tubes by Bocour Artists Colors, 552 West 52 St., New York 19, N.Y., and available at art supply stores.

Masonite—a commercial, pressed fiber board available at building suppliers. Tempered Masonite has a hard finish; untempered, a soft finish.

matte medium—a painting medium which dries to a flat, non-glare finish.

matte varnish—a final varnish which will not cloud over dark colors and which dries flat. It may also be used as a medium.

medium—the basic liquid binder into which powdered pigments are ground to make a paint. A vehicle. (Plural: media.) Mediums or various media may be used with and added to a paint to modify its properties.

methyl isobutyl ketone—a highly toxic solvent used to dissolve and thin some of the synthetic paint resins and solutions. Available at chemical suppliers.

mezzotint—printing technique in which carborundum is rubbed between two copper plates to create a rough grain on the copper. The rough copper is polished (burnished) with a piece of steel to create white areas of the design when the plate is inked, wiped, and printed; rough areas produce soft gradations of black to gray.

migration of plasticizer—some of the synthetics (notably the polyvinyls) require chemicals called plasticizers to make them flexible. Many of these plasticizers are deficient in that they sink into the support upon which the paint is applied, or they evaporate. This process in which the plasticizer leaves the paint film is called migration; the paint is left brittle as a result. The length of time a plasticizer takes to migrate varies.

mineral spirits—a volatile thinner used to thin oils and some of the synthetic resins. It is a rectified petroleum product, varies in quality from brand to brand, and dries somewhat faster than turpentine.

modeling paste—in relation to the polymer emulsions, a product made by adding marble dust and other inert material to the polymer medium producing a heavy bodied "paste" which can be used for impasto and modeling and sculptural techniques.

monomer—the thin, volatile, relatively simple molecular chemical units which are polymerized into non-volatile, solid, and extremely stable polymers.

monoprint—a print taken from a surface which will produce only one print copy. A water-base paint is usually painted onto a repellent surface (such as glass) and paper is placed over the design to make the print.

Nacconal NRSF—a wetting agent which helps the dispersion of pigments in aqueous media. Produced by National Aniline Division of Allied Chemical Corp., Somerville, Mass., or Allied Chemical Corp., New York, N.Y.

New Masters—a copolymer emulsion paint line packaged in plastic tubes and bottles by California Products Corp., 169 Waverly St., Cambridge 39, Mass., and available in art supply stores.

nitrocellulose—cellulose fiber which has been nitrated by drastic treatment with nitric acid. It is soluble in certain organic solvents, and, with modification with flexiblizing plasticizers and with various resins, it makes the well known nitrocellulose lacquers (known also as pyroxylin lacquers). While nitrocellulose lacquers are tough and relatively durable for moderate periods of time, their nitrated structure will eventually cause film disintegration.

organic solvents—chemical liquids that are compounds of carbon and, as referred to in this book, evaporate. They are solvents for (i.e., they dissolve) resins and nitrocellulose. The term usually applies to the stronger or more active solvents such as acetone, tuluol, xylene, ethyl acetate, butanol, methyl isobutyl ketone, etc., rather than the more common and weaker organic solvents such as turpentine and mineral spirits.

oxidation—a chemical action in which a material combines with oxygen. Oils dry by the process of oxidation; a chemical drying process.

paint—a combination of medium (binder, vehicle) and pigment.

papier-mâché—a construction or material made by mixing a binder with paper pulp or paper cuttings.

Perlite—expanded mica. A very light-weight material which can be used for textural additives in paint. It is obtainable at building suppliers.

pigment—a dry, powder substance which imparts its color to a medium but which is not dissolved in the medium. Pigments may be either derived from natural sources or produced chemically, synthetically. (See Appendix, Part I.) Source: art supply stores and companies, and pigment supply companies.

plasticizers—substances which are added to a medium to maintain necessary flexibility or to correct undesirable brittleness.

Plexiglas—acrylic plastic manufactured by Rohm and Haas, Inc., Philadelphia, Penn.

Politec—an acrylic emulsion paint produced in jars by José Gutiérrez, Calle Tigre No. 24, Mexico 12, D.F., and distributed in the United States by the Politec Co., 425 14th St., San Francisco, Calif.

polymer—a compound formed by chemically uniting a number of like molecules into larger molecules and thereby changing the physical properties of the basic compounds (monomers) without altering its essential composition. Volatile monomers are polymerized into non-volatile and extremely stable polymers.

polymer cement—a sculptural medium made by mixing polymer emulsion with cement and other additives. See Part II, Chapter 15, *As a Medium for Sculpture.*

polymer emulsion—a water suspension of a synthetic resin to form a paint medium which can suspend pigments in a liquid state, and, upon drying, keep the pigment dispersed as well as protected. "Synthetic emulsion" and "polymer tempera" are terms used to mean the same thing.

polymerization—the process by which a polymer is made. See polymer.

polymer tempera—see polymer emulsion.

Polymer Tempera—the polymer emulsion medium developed by Alfred Duca. (See Part II, Chapter 15, for uses and formula.) This medium is a polyvinyl acetate emulsion and has to be formulated by the artist and is not available on the market. It was the first commercial polymer emulsion produced for the artist.

polyvinyl acetate (PVA)—a plastic resin of the vinyl family which requires a plasticizer to make it flexible. Vinyl acetate is polymerized by adding peroxides and heating to yield polyvinyl acetate emulsions.

Polyvinyl Acetate Emulsion 953-7 A (Polyco 953-7 A)—a PVA emulsion manufactured by the Borden Co., Chemical Division, Foster St., Peabody, Mass. This is the PVA used to make *Polymer Tempera.*

polyesters—a class of synthetic resins which frequently are cast *in situ* at normal temperatures, activated by small percentage of catalyst. The catalyst is usually volatile and highly toxic.

priming—a coating of white paint (usually white lead) applied to a sized canvas to provide a base for painting as well as for a reflective surface in oil painting. The priming can also be one of synthetic emulsion gesso. The oil priming should not be painted over for four weeks after its application; the

synthetic priming can be painted over with oils as soon as it is dry (about twenty minutes). A size must be used with oil priming. No size is required with synthetic priming.

pumice—powdered, volcanic-type rock used for polishing materials and for textural additives in painting and collagraphy. Available at large building suppliers, some paint and pigment suppliers.

pyroxylin—see nitrocellulose.

resin—an organic substance exuded from plants or trees which can be dissolved in volatile solvents to produce a paint medium or varnish which is transparent and water resistant. Resins may be hard or soft, recent (extracted from living trees) or fossil (those dug from the earth, such as copal). Synthetic resins are substances which have properties similar to those in natural resins, but which are made by chemical processes; such as the plastic resins discussed in this book.

resin solution—a resin dissolved in a volatile thinner or organic solvent. Resin solutions are not compatible with water or aqueous media.

Resoflex (R-296)—an excellent plasticizer and the only one to be used in the formulation of *Polymer Tempera.* Resoflex R-296 is a product of Cambridge Industries, Cambridge, Mass.

Rhoplex AC 33 and AC 34—types of acrylic emulsions produced by Rohm and Haas Co., Philadelphia, Penn. Small quantities can be obtained through their distributors (such as Masco Chemical Co., 58 John Hay Ave., Kearny, N.J.)

serigraph—a fine art, silk-screen process in which designs are made on silk. Color is scraped over the design with a squeegee so the color will print through areas of the silk which have not been blocked out. The technique is a multi-color, multi-screen process which resembles gouache painting. The effects achieved can be very subtle and varied.

Shiva Acrylic—an acrylic emulsion paint line produced in tubes by Shiva

Artists Colors, Shiva-Rhodes Building, 10th and Monroe Streets, Paducah, Kentucky. Available at art supply stores.

silica—white or colorless and extremely hard silicon dioxides and the principal constituent of sand, quartz, etc. Silicates referred to in this book are the crystalline, inert pigments with little or no tinting strength used to give body or impart tooth to a medium.

silicon esters—volatile liquid, organic compounds of silica, among which is ethyl silicate.

silverpoint—a drawing technique which uses a piece of silver to draw on a coated paper to produce a pale, delicate gray line. The Old Masters used this technique and coated their papers with a thin colored ground of powdered bone, mixed with gum water. Today the coating can be synthetic emulsion gesso.

size—a coating given to raw canvas before the priming. It protects the canvas from the harmful effects of the oil paints and gives the canvas a heavier body. An animal glue (or glue gelatine) is used for this purpose.

spackling compound—a plaster-like compound used to patch cracked masonry, plaster, murals, etc., and which can be used to create impasto surfaces when mixed with the polymer emulsions. Source: paint stores and building suppliers.

stabilizer—a chemical used to keep many of the synthetic emulsions in suspension.

stand oil—a thickened linseed oil made by heating the oil in stainless metal containers at a high temperature in the absence of oxygen. It does not yellow as much as linseed oil. Source: art supply stores.

Styrofoam—a plastic produced by the Dow Chemical Co. and available at building suppliers and plastic supply houses.

solution media—painting media made by dissolving resins in volatile thinners.

sun-thickened linseed oil—a thick

linseed oil made by exposing the oil in shallow pans to the sun. This process gradually thickens the oil, bleaches it and gives it faster drying properties. It is the best and fastest drying of the oils and does not yellow as much as linseed oil; it flows better and gives brighter and more transparent colors for oil painting. Source: art supply stores. Permanent Pigments, Inc., 2700 Highland Ave., Norwood 12, Ohio, produces the only sun-thickened oil colors available.

support—the surface material upon which paint is applied; the canvas, Masonite, board, or paper to which the size and then priming are applied.

synthetic emulsion—see polymer emulsion.

synthetic paint—a paint based on synthetic resin media; either emulsion or solution types.

tempera—a painting medium using either animal (egg) or vegetable (gums such as gum arabic) glues diluted with water—as an emulsion—into which are mixed powdered pigments to form a paint.

toluene (toluol)—see volatile solvents. Source: large paint stores and chemical suppliers.

tooth—a slight roughness of the surface.

toxic thinners—see volatile thinners.

Tri-Tec—an oil-wax-casein emulsion paint which is thinned with water. Produced by Permanent Pigments, Inc., 2700 Highland Ave., Norwood 12, Ohio, and available at art supply stores.

turpentine—distilled gum of pine trees. See volatile solvents.

underpainting—the basic structure or design of the painting which may be done broadly or in high detail, in black and white, complementary colors, etc., before the final painting or "finish" takes place.

varnish—a solution or emulsion medium for coating finished paintings so they

will withstand dampness, grease, dust and atmospheric as well as chemical damage. They are available in matte and gloss finishes for all media.

vehicle—the medium (either traditional or synthetic) used to "carry" the pigment and other ingredients to make a paint. See also binder, medium.

Venice turpentine—an oil-type medium (balsam) from the European larch tree. It gives adhesion and a high gloss when mixed with oil mediums. It was used by the Old Masters as a thickening agent and for special oil recipes, but is little used today.

Vermiculite—expanded mica. A lightweight additive used for textural painting and for use as an aggregate in sculpture. Available at building suppliers.

vinyl—a type of synthetic resin used to make the synthetic paints. Vinyl is usually brittle in paint formulations and requires plasticizers.

vinyl acetate—plastic resin made by adding acetylene to acetic acid in the presence of mercury salts. There are many types of vinyl acetate and vinyl chloride acetates; most have poor adhesion properties, can only be used in thin (low solids content) media and are not very resistant to ultraviolet light (so that they have to be loaded with ultraviolet "absorbers" as well as plasticizers). The artist should be sure of the type he uses to avoid these handicaps as much as possible. See Vinylite.

vinyl chloride acetate—a copolymer resin (vinyl chloride—vinyl acetate) which comes as white fluffy powders and must be dissolved in high volatile thinners. See vinyl acetate and Vinylite.

Vinylite (AYAF and AYAT)—vinyl acetate resins produced by Union Carbide Corp., 270 Park Ave., New York, N.Y., (Chemicals Division) and available at chemical suppliers or distributors.

Vinylite (VMCH and VYHH)—vinyl chloride acetate resins. Source: same as above.

Vinylseal—a solution of vinyl acetate (dissolved in acetone) which is produced by Union Carbide Corp. (See above.)

volatile thinners or solvents—liquids that completely evaporate from the paint film and usually have pungent, characteristic odors. They are inflammable and frequently highly toxic to the human body if steadily inhaled in high concentration. Acetone, benzene, toluene, xylene and lacquer thinners are the stronger solvents which should only be used in well ventilated areas. Turpentine and mineral spirits are volatile solvents with which all artists are well acquainted and are low in toxicity. They are all used to dissolve resins to make paint solutions or to thin mediums or paints. Available from art supply stores, paint stores, or chemical suppliers.

watercolor—an aqueous medium of water and gum arabic into which powdered pigments are ground. Sometimes a plasticizer such as glycerin is used in the paint.

wetting agent—a chemical used in paints to help pigments become "wet" or easily dispersed and ground into the medium.

xylene—see volatile solvent.

INDEX